PHL

D1391276

THE
PAUL HAMLYN
LIBRARY

DONATED BY
THE PAUL HAMLYN
FOUNDATION
TO THE
BRITISH MUSEUM

opened December 2000

THE HOUSE OF HORUS AT EDFU

Ritual in an Ancient Egyptian Temple

THE HOUSE OF HORUS AT EDFU

Ritual in an Ancient Egyptian Temple

Barbara Watterson

TEMPUS

For Alice

First published 1998

Published by:
Tempus Publishing Limited
The Mill, Brimscombe Port
Stroud, Gloucestershire, GL5 2QG

© Barbara Watterson, 1998

The right of Barbara Watterson to be identified as the Author
of this work has been asserted by her in accordance with the
Copyrights, Designs and Patents Act 1988.

Typesetting and origination by Tempus Publishing Ltd.
Printed and bound in Great Britain.

All rights reserved. No part of this book may be reprinted or reproduced or
utilised in any form or by any electronic, mechanical or other means, now
known or hereafter invented, including photocopying and recording, or in any
information storage or retrieval system, without the permission in writing from
the Publishers.

British Library Cataloguing in Publication Data.
A catalogue record for this book is available from the British Library.

ISBN 07524 1405 4

299.31 WAT

Contents

List of Illustrations

Colour plates (between pages 64 and 65)

Chronological Table

PREDYNASTIC PERIOD	*c.* 5500-*c.* 3100 BC	
DYNASTIC PERIOD	*c.* 3100 BC-30 BC	
SELECTED KINGS	**Reign**	

Dynasty III
Djoser — *c.* 2667-2648 BC

Dynasty V
Unas — *c.* 2377-2347 BC

Dynasty VI — *c.* 2345-2181 BC

Dynasty XVIII
Hatshepsut — 1479-1457 BC
Thutmose III — 1479-1425 BC

Dynasty XIX
Sety I — 1294-1279 BC
Ramesses II — 1279-1213 BC

Dynasty XX
Ramesses III — 1184-1153 BC

Dynasty XXX
Nectanebo II — 360-343 BC

Dynasty XXXI
Darius III Codomannus — 336-332 BC

Dynasty XXXII

King		**Queen**
Alexander the Great	332-323 BC	Roxane, Statiera
Philip Arrhidaeus	323-316 BC	
Alexander IV	316-304 BC	
Ptolemy I Soter I	304-284 BC	Artacama (d. of Artabazus of

		Persia) Eurydice (d. of Antipater of Macedon) Berenice I
Ptolemy II Philadelphus	282-246 BC	Arsinoe I (d. of Lysimachus of Thrace & Nicaea) Arsinoe II (d. of Ptolemy I & Berenice I)
Ptolemy III Euergetes I	246-221 BC	Berenice II (d. of Magas of Cyrenaica)
Ptolemy IV Philopator	221-205 BC	Arsinoe III (d. of Ptolemy III & Berenice II)
Ptolemy V Epiphanes	205-180 BC	Cleopatra I (d. of Antiochus of Syria)
Ptolemy VI Philometor	180-145 BC	Cleopatra II (d. of Ptolemy V & Cleopatra I)
Ptolemy VII Neos Philopator	145 BC	
Ptolemy VIII Euergetes II (Physkon)	170-116 BC	Cleopatra II (d. of Ptolemy V & Cleopatra I) Cleopatra III (d. of Ptolemy VI & Cleopatra II)
Ptolemy IX Soter II (Lathyros)	116-80 BC	Cleopatra IV (d. of Ptolemy VIII & Cleopatra III) Cleopatra V Selene (d. of Ptolemy VIII &

		Cleopatra III)
Cleopatra III, joint ruler with her son Ptolemy IX	116-101 BC	
Ptolemy X Alexander I, joint ruler with his mother Cleopatra III and his brother Ptolemy IX	110-101 BC	Berenice III (d. of Ptolemy IX & Cleopatra V)
joint ruler with brother	101-88 BC	
Ptolemy XI Alexander II	80 BC	Berenice II, his stepmother, widow of Ptolemy X
Ptolemy XII Neos Dionysos	80-51 BC	Cleopatra VI Tryphania (d. of Ptolemy IX and a mistress
Berenice IV	58-55 BC	
Ptolemy XIII	51-47 BC	Cleopatra VII (sister)
Ptolemy XIV	47-44 BC	Cleopatra VII (sister)
Cleopatra VII	51-30 BC	Married Marcus Antonius (in 41 BC), by whom she had twins, Alexander Helios & Cleopatra Selene (born 40 BC) and Ptolemy Philadelphus (born 35 BC)
Ptolemy XV Caesarion (son of Julius Caesar and Cleopatra VII, born 47 BC)	44-30 BC	

Glossary

Calendar	the ancient Egyptians used a solar not a lunar calendar, dividing the civil year into 12 months of 30 days each. Five *epagomenal* days (*see* below) brought it up to 365. The extra quarter of a day each year was not taken into account, with the result that the civil year gradually became out of step with the astonomical year
cartouche	oval inside which a king's name was written
cavetto cornice	curved ornamental moulding at the top of a wall
Copt, Coptic	native Egyptians of the Graeco-Roman period onwards; from sixteenth century AD referred specifically to Christian Egyptians
Dynasty	one of the divisions into which the kings of Egypt were divided by the scholar-priest Manetho in the third century BC
Ennead	group of nine deities (from Greek meaning 'set of nine')
epagomenal days	the five days added on to the Egyptian year of 360 days (from Greek *epagomenal* meaning 'added')
hieroglyphs	picture-writing of ancient Egypt. Word derived from Greek *hieros* (sacred) *glupho* (sculptures)
Nomes	Greek term for the administrative districts into which Egypt had been divided since the beginning of history, and which eventually numbered twenty-two in the south (Upper Egypt) and twenty in the north (Lower Egypt)
predynastic	period of Egyptian history that predates writing and the unification of Egypt; the prehistoric period before 3100 BC
pylon gateway	monumental gateway at the entrance to an Egyptian temple
satrap	governor of a province in ancient Persian times
temenos	sacred precinct of a temple
Thebaïd	district in which the ancient Egyptian 'City of Amun' (modern Luxor) was situated; called Thebes by the Greeks, hence Thebaïd
torus roll	semi-circular moulding at top or side edges of walls

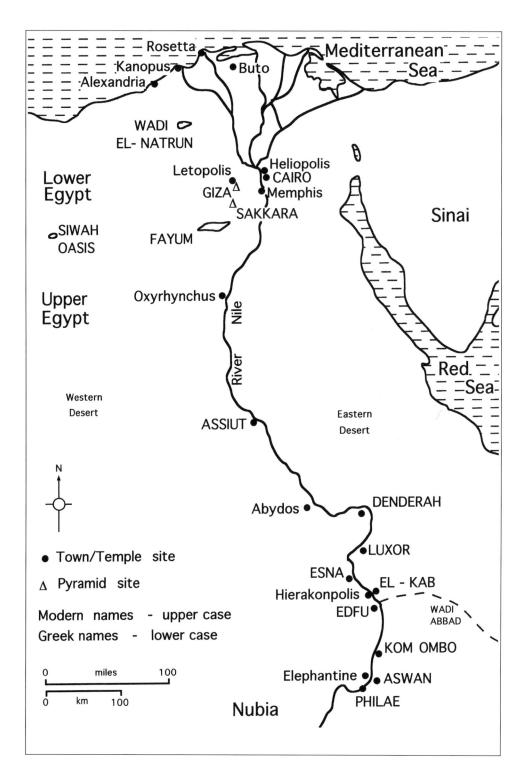

Fig. 1   Map of Egypt

1 The Historical Background

For over two thousand years Egypt was ruled by successive dynasties of Egyptian kings; but from the beginning of the first millennium BC the country was subjected to invasions, first by Libyans, then by Nubians and Persians. The first Persian occupation, during which Egypt, Cyrenaica in Libya and the oases in the Western Desert became the Sixth Satrapy or Governorate of the Persian Empire, ended in revolt; but by 341 BC, the last native-born King of Egypt, Nectanebo II (360-343 BC), had abdicated, and an old Hebrew prophecy was fulfilled: 'There shall be no more a prince out of the land of Egypt.' The Persian occupation was different from the others. Libyans and Nubians had seized the political initiative but preserved the basic framework of Egyptian society, and adopted the culture of Egypt as their own, claiming the throne of Egypt, styling themselves Kings of Egypt and undertaking the traditional duties and responsibilities of the office. The Persians deprived the Egyptians of their independence and there were no more kings of Egypt; instead the country was ruled by a representative of the Persian King, a satrap based in Memphis.

Egypt remained under Persian rule until the reign of Darius III (336-332 BC), who came to the throne of Persia in the year that Philip II, King of Macedon, died and was succeeded by his son, Alexander III, known today as Alexander the Great (336-323 BC). Philip of Macedon had become king in 359 BC at the age of twenty-three and immediately set about persuading the city-states of Greece to unite - under his leadership, naturally. His campaign to win over the city-states lasted for over twenty years, and it was not until he had defeated the Athenians at the Battle of Chaeronea in 338 BC that Philip became Supreme Commander, ready to lead the united armies of Greece against its greatest enemy, Persia. All seemed to be progressing well: the Oracle at Delphi, asked if the Persian campaign would be successful, had seemingly favoured Philip's cause; the expeditionary force sent to the Greek colonies on the western coast of Asia Minor, Ionia, had been welcomed; and there were revolts in Egypt against the Persians. In Susa, so it was rumoured, the Grand Vizier, Bagoas, had poisoned not only the reigning king but his successor also, and by 336 BC the untried Darius III, who was not of the old royal family, sat on the throne of Persia.

In that year Philip arranged a marriage between his daughter, Cleopatra, and her uncle, Alexander, King of Epirus (Albania). The marriage took place at Aigai in the oldest Macedonian palace and the celebrations went on for several days. On the last day of the wedding feast, Philip took part in a procession to the theatre in which statues of the twelve gods of Olympus, and one of Philip himself, an innovation that many considered hubristic, were carried. Philip had decreed that it would not be fitting for him to walk to the theatre with his bodyguard, and instead was escorted by his son, Alexander, and his son-in-law, Alexander, King of Epirus. By the theatre entrance, Pausanias, a young bodyguard, lay in wait; and as Philip passed by sprang out and stabbed him to death. Pausanias tried to escape but was killed by the other bodyguards before he could reveal whether he had been acting alone or on someone else's instructions. Suspicion fell on Philip's estranged wife, Olympias. She had not attended the wedding; but she immediately travelled to Aigai and, having had Pausanias' body taken down from the stake to which it had been tied, burned it on a funeral pyre built over that of her husband.

Philip of Macedon had at least seven wives. Olympias was the most powerful. She was a princess of Epirus who claimed that she was descended from Achilles, one of Greece's greatest heroes in the Trojan War; and that the blood of Helen of Troy ran in her veins. Since Helen was said to be the daughter of Leda, queen of Sparta, and the King of the Gods, Zeus, who had seduced her in the guise of a swan, Olympias was thereby claiming a modicum of divinity. As an orphan, she was under the care of her uncle, the King of Epirus, who because his kingdom abutted Macedon's western border was a desirable ally for Philip. His marriage to Olympias, which probably took place in 357 BC, was thus a political union, although there was a rumour that when Olympias was being initiated on the island of Samothrace into the mysteries of an obscure religious cult in which demons of the Underworld were worshipped, her eyes met those of an onlooker who was immediately attracted to her. The onlooker, surprisingly, was Philip, not known for his interest in obscure religious mysteries.

Olympias was a very forceful woman, quarrelsome, ruthless and not averse to having perceived rivals murdered. She was intensely interested in mystery religions and, like the Macedonians, was a devotee of Dionysus, the god of wine. As a maenad or priestess of Dionysus she was famed for handling snakes during the Dionysian rites that she led when she was Queen of Macedon, a practice she had brought with her from Dodona, her birthplace in Epirus, where snakes were worshipped. Olympias' greatest claim to fame was that she was the mother of Philip's heir, his only viable legitimate son, Alexander. He was born in 356 BC, less than a year after his mother's marriage to Philip: even so, Olympias did not hesitate to hint that her son's father was not the King of Macedon but the King of the Gods, Zeus himself. Olympias never gave details of Alexander's conception, but she did claim that Zeus ordered the goddess, Artemis, to leave her sanctuary at Ephesus in order to supervise his son's birth; and Alexander's official birthday was 6th July, the day dedicated to Artemis. When the Temple of Artemis caught fire it was claimed to be because the goddess was absent on midwifery duties. A story less flattering to Olympias was told by the Persians, who claimed Alexander as their own after his death, saying that Olympias had paid a secret visit to the

Persian court where the King impregnated her only to send her home immediately afterwards because of her bad breath!

On the death of Philip, Alexander inherited the throne of a Macedon that, thanks to his father's efforts, was rich and flourishing. He also inherited the leadership of the Greek city-states and his father's ambition to defeat Persia. He was twenty years old and destined to become one of the world's most famous men. Surprisingly little is known about him. Surviving descriptions of his appearance were all written posthumously and either derived from his statues or portraits, or written with an eye to proving a point. He was never painted 'warts and all'[1] and as an adult he would only sit to be painted by Apelles, sculpted by Lysippus or carved on gems by Pyrgoteles, court artists who produced stylized portraits.

Later legend claimed that Alexander had odd-coloured eyes, the left black, the right blue-green. He was famous for the liquid intensity of his gaze, of which he made good use, bending it upon anyone he spoke to. In his portraits he is shown gazing upwards, possibly to indicate divinity although if he were as short in stature as is often claimed, this might have been his normal stance when forced to look up to speak to those taller than he. He is also shown with his head and neck turned to one side, this again due probably to this being his 'listening' stance rather than an indication of a wry-neck caused by a wound or infirmity, which the official portraits would never have shown. Alexander's height is a matter of speculation, but it is known that when he sat upon the throne of Persia he needed a small table to rest his feet on rather than a footstool.

There is agreement that the skin on Alexander's body was white although his face was a weatherbeaten red. A fellow-pupil of his tutor, Aristotle, made a point of noting that Alexander's body was sweet-smelling, an indication perhaps that he liked to use perfumed ointments. He was clean-shaven, which was unusual at the time; and his hair stood up from his brow and fell into a central parting. It was long, in contrast to the close-cropped military style generally in favour; and may have been fair, or even red-gold. If so, this would account for the colour of his skin — the paleness typical of a red-head — and the lack of a beard — a red, possibly sparse, beard may have been considered unbecoming. It could even account for the length of his hair, grown to show off its colour and to make Alexander appear like the sun-god, Apollo. He was said to have had a leonine look. Above all, he had presence.

Alexander had his father's ambition and capacity for organization; but whereas Philip was patient and cautious, often devious, always planning ahead, Alexander had a short temper and could be rash and headstrong, especially when he was drunk. As he grew older his drinking increased, its worst consequence being his burning of the great Persian city of Persepolis, reputedly on the whim of Thaïs, a courtesan. He was ruthless: he had his baby half-brother killed in case he became a rival; and had Thebes sacked, and all its inhabitants killed or sold into slavery, because the city had threatened to withdraw its support of him. Alexander walked and talked very rapidly, was prepared to take risks and liked to settle problems by immediate action. In Phrygia, he was told about Gordius, a peasant who, having been made king by Zeus, had dedicated his wagon to the god and tied its yoke to a beam with a knot of such intricacy that it could not be untied. Alexander was informed that 'whoever undid the knot would reign over the whole East' and solved the problem of how to untie the Gordian knot by slicing it into two with his sword, not quite what was meant by untying the knot but effective. In contrast, he sat as a boy of only twelve years of age patiently observing his father's grooms trying to master a wonderful Akhal-Teke horse from Turkmenistan, a breed notoriously difficult to train. They failed largely because they had not noticed that the horse was balking at its own shadow. Alexander turned the horse to face the sun and rode him successfully, winning him as a present from his father. Alexander was to ride the great Bucephalas in almost every battle he fought until the horse was killed in India at the Battle of Jhelum in 324 BC.

In 334 BC Alexander crossed the Hellespont at the head of 35,000 men. His army defeated the Persians in battle at Granicus, a river east of Troy, and King Darius fled the battlefield. The cities of Asia Minor welcomed Alexander who went on to defeat the Persians again in 333 BC, this time at Issus, east of the Taurus mountains. After the battle, Darius' wife and children were taken captive and Darius proposed peace but could not bring himself to meet Alexander's demand that he come in person to discuss it. Alexander marched into Phoenicia and captured Damascus and, by August 332 BC, all the cities on the Mediterranean coast; and Darius offered to ransom his family for 10,000 talents, probably equivalent to seven million pounds sterling today, and to cede to Alexander all of Asia west of the Euphrates. He also offered a marriage alliance with his daughter. Alexander refused. Alexander's third and final defeat of Darius took place at Gaugamela, east of the Tigris river in Mesopotamia, in July 331 BC, after which he went on to capture Persia itself. Darius was murdered in Bactria (Afghanistan) the following year.

Alexander's final battle against Darius could have taken place nearly a year earlier than it did. The logical move after capturing Phoenicia would have been to continue eastwards into Mesopotamia and thence perhaps to Persia. Alexander chose to divert part of his army to Egypt. Some scholars have explained this interlude as a breathing-space before the last great push to Persia; or even as a sign that Alexander had not made up his mind whether he wanted to attack Persia itself. Egypt made a contribution to the Persian treasury with a yearly tribute of 700 talents, about half a million pounds sterling today, but it was on the periphery of the Persian Empire and its capture was not necessary to Alexander's overall plan of campaign.

Alexander arrived in Egypt in October 332 BC and departed seven months later in April 331. During the years of foreign invasions, the Greeks had come to the aid of the Egyptians on several occasions; this time they came as liberators and drove the Persians out of Egypt almost without striking a blow. The arrival of the glorious Alexander, with his fame, his success and even his glamour and the romance attached to his name, must have been regarded by most Egyptians as a gift from the gods, a way by which the country could regain its freedom and reestablish the natural order of things as it had done after each previous period of foreign domination. Sadly for the Egyptians, Alexander's arrival simply marked the beginning of the end of ancient Egyptian civilization.

To the Persians, as in later years to the Romans, Egypt had been not much more than a milch cow, or rather a gigantic granary from which to extract wheat and barley. In contrast, Alexander always paid great attention to the culture and customs of the countries he conquered. In Memphis on 14 November 332, he allowed himself to be crowned king in the Egyptian fashion, by Egyptian priests, thus, according to Egyptian tradition, becoming a god. He made offerings to Egyptian deities and ordered the temples at Karnak and Luxor to be repaired. Above all he ordered the foundation of the first, and greatest, of the cities that bore his name, Alexandria. Although the official foundation of Alexandria was dated to 7 April 331 BC, Alexander had chosen the site on the north-western coast of Egypt in January of that year, marking out its ground-plan himself. Having done so, he was, according to his biographer Arrian, 'seized with a longing to visit Ammon in Siwah' and in February set out on the arduous three-week-long trek across more than 300 miles (500km) of the Western Desert to the Siwah Oasis to consult the famous Oracle of Zeus Ammon.

Even today, Siwah is so isolated that its inhabitants do not consider themselves Egyptian, but Alexander was prepared to devote six weeks of his time to making the pilgrimage which may have been the object of his detour to Egypt. He consulted the Oracle but his question, and the answer it received, he kept to himself, saying only that the Oracle had told him what his heart desired. According to Egyptian belief, Alexander would have gone to Siwah to be recognized by the state god, Amun (Ammon), as his son, theogamy (the practice of the state god begetting a child upon the wife of an earthly king) being one way in which a king validated his claim to the Egyptian throne. From Alexander's point of view, the Oracle may have reassured him of his legitimacy, for the story told by Olympias about his divine parentage (*see* p.16) may have sown doubt in his mind that he was indeed the son of Philip of Macedon.

Alexander wrote to his mother that he would tell her and her alone what the Oracle had said when he could do so in person; but he was destined never to go back to Macedon and never saw Olympias again. Eight years after consulting the Oracle at Siwah, on 13 June 323, Alexander lay dead in Babylon. His empire was divided among his generals who ruled it as satraps during the reigns of his half-brother, Philip Arrhidaeus, who was murdered in 316 BC, and Alexander's posthumous son, Alexander IV, murdered in 304 BC. Once Alexander's heirs had been disposed of, however, the erstwhile satraps lost no time in declaring themselves kings of their respective countries.

If Alexander had not defeated the Persians, Egypt would have remained on the periphery of the Persian Empire. If the Greeks had been led by anyone other than Alexander, who valued Egypt for his own personal reasons, it might have remained a backwater. But Alexander had conquered Egypt without a battle, he had been welcomed by the people because of his reputation and by the priests, who exercised a great deal of influence, because of his willingness to accept the dictates of Egyptian religion. Shortly after his death, if not before, they were claiming that Nectanebo II (*see* p.15) had assumed the shape of a serpent in order to impregnate Olympias, thus making Alexander the true heir to the throne of Egypt. Above all, Alexander had founded Alexandria with the intention that the city should be a great centre of commerce and trade, the intellectual capital of the Hellenistic world and the link between east and west. It was not Egypt, however, that was considered the choice prize after Alexander's death when his generals were dividing his empire among themselves.

Egypt fell to Ptolemy, whose parentage, like that of Alexander himself, had been questioned. Ptolemy's father, Lagus, was an obscure Macedonian squire whose wife, Ptolemy's mother, was a princess of the Macedonian royal family and above Lagus' station. It was rumoured that she had been married off to Lagus because she was pregnant with Philip of Macedon's child. Whatever the truth of this rumour, Philip always took an interest in Ptolemy and made him one of the young Alexander's seven Companions, boys selected to be brought up and educated alongside the prince. When Alexander left Macedon on his 'Great Adventure', Ptolemy went with him and fought in the ensuing campaigns with great distinction, becoming master of the horse. As a member of the royal bodyguard, he was one of Alexander's most trusted advisors.

Ptolemy may or may not have been Alexander's illegitimate half-brother, but he had Alexander's talent for making use of the customs of other countries. When Alexander died, Ptolemy was astute enough to wrest his body from the other generals and take it not to Macedon, Alexander's birthplace, or to Persia, but to Egypt. Alexander was at first interred in Memphis, which the Egyptians took as a great compliment, though Ptolemy may have intended the final burial place to be at Siwah. However, both he and Alexander were eventually buried in the great tomb, the Sema, that was prepared for Alexander in Alexandria. By burying Alexander, Ptolemy was acting in accordance with an ancient Egyptian tradition in which a dead king was buried by his successor just as the mythical God-King, Osiris, had been buried by his son, Horus. Every living King of Egypt was regarded as a Horus, every dead king as an Osiris, and since it was the act of burial that conferred legitimacy upon the new king, he need not necessarily be a son of his predecessor. By acting as Horus to Alexander's Osiris, Ptolemy was gaining the right to claim the throne of Egypt although, for the present, he was content to remain a satrap.

Egypt was a good choice on Ptolemy's part. He must have realized that before long the ambitions of the other satraps would bring them into conflict with one another. He himself had been awarded Egypt with permisssion to expand his territory to the west 'by the spear'; the other satraps would doubtless try to extend their territories 'by the spear' by attacking their neighbours. Egypt was not contiguous with other satrapies; and its great wealth would enable Ptolemy to maintain an army large enough to secure his position and to create an adequate buffer state in western Asia. The shrewd Ptolemy may also have calculated that Egypt, a country that had welcomed Alexander not as a conqueror but as a liberator, might prove to be easier to govern than the vanquished satrapies, especially by Ptolemy himself, who had rid the land of a bad Persian satrap, and was, therefore, popular with the Egyptians.

Ptolemy needed to consolidate his position in Egypt. He could not be certain that he would be left alone by his erstwhile Companions to govern Egypt in peace, and needed a contented and loyal country to maintain him and to recognise him as ruler. Unlike Alexander, he could not claim to be of divine descent in order to legitimize his occupation of the throne in the eyes of his Egyptian subjects. He could have done so by marrying an Egyptian princess of royal descent, but he chose not to, as did his successors. He proclaimed himself king in 304 BC as Ptolemy Soter (Saviour); and allowed his name to be enclosed in a *cartouche* (*see* Glossary) in inscriptions, styling himself 'Ptulmis, beloved of Amun and son of Re'.

During his reign, Ptolemy was inevitably drawn into the quarrels and wars between the other satraps/kings, but succeeded in conquering Cyprus and Palestine and acquiring large tracts of land in the Aegean and Asia Minor. Alexandria became one of the richest cities in the world, partly through its busy port and partly through the manufacture and export of glass, linen and papyrus. It also became the supreme centre for learning and scholarship in the ancient world, attracting philosophers, scientists and men of literature who came to the city to study at the Academy of the Muses or Mouseion (Museum), founded by Ptolemy Soter, which, thanks to his careful management of the Egyptian economy, they did at state expense.

Alexandria was considered to be in but not of Egypt and was treated differently from the rest of the country. In conformity with Alexander's wish that it should be an Hellenic city run in a democratic manner, every male Macedonian or Greek inhabitant was a citizen with the right to bear arms and to meet and discuss political matters in open assembly. These rights did not extend to its Jewish or Egyptian inhabitants. Ptolemy Soter had no intention of allowing Alexandria to develop into a city-state, and so, although its citizens were allowed to carry arms, they were not permitted to use them; and the assembly chamber was a mere forum for debate without any political powers. Government was in the hands of the king; and, as long as Ptolemy Soter was king, it was governed well. He was a more than able administrator and was responsible for drawing up the main lines of the Ptolemaic administrative, legal and military systems that on the whole worked well.

Ptolemy Soter set the pattern for the dynasty in his treatment of Egypt, which was regarded as the king's private domain. He administered the country ruthlessly, though efficiently, fully exploiting its resources. In an attempt to provide his Greek and Egyptian subjects with a common interest, he introduced a new god to the pantheon. This was Serapis, whose name is a combination of the names of two ancient Egyptian deities, User (Greek: Osiris), King of the

Underworld, and Hapy (Greek: Apis), the sacred bull of Memphis. Serapis was a hybrid of the Egyptian Osiris and the Greek gods Zeus, Dionysus and Asklepios, the god of healing whom the Greeks identified with the enormously popular Egyptian, Imhotep (*see* p.46). Thus Serapis was a deity of the Underworld and of fertility, a helper of mankind with the attributes of a physician. Ptolemy Soter had a great temple built for his new god in Rhakotis, the quarter in Alexandria inhabited by native Egyptians. The temple, the Serapeum, became a place of pilgrimage; Serapis, however, appealed to Greek tastes and was never fully accepted by the Egyptians. He proved popular in Greece, and later in Rome, and the Ptolemies were able to make use of his popularity, and the even greater popularity of the native Egyptian goddess, Isis, to promulgate Egyptian culture in the Hellenistic world.

Ptolemy Soter was the only one of Alexander's generals to die an old man, peacefully, in his own bed. At the time of his death, around 282 BC, he had taken no active part in affairs of state for two or three years, leaving the government of Egypt in the hands of his son, Ptolemy II Philadelphus (282-246 BC). Philadelphus (The Brother-loving God) was only twenty-three years old when his father retired, but the old king obviously had every confidence in his son's abilities. He founded Greek settlements throughout Egypt, especially in the Fayum, which was extensively developed and renamed, after his wife, the Arsinoite district. Philadelphus had the ancient canal linking the Nile with the Red Sea reopened and actively promoted Red Sea trade; and it was in his reign that the Ptolemaic financial system was organized. Above all, Philadelphus paid great attention to Alexandria. His two most impressive additions to the city were the Lighthouse built on the island of Pharos, which was to become one of the Seven Wonders of the World; and the Library. He had the Great Library built in the Brucheion quarter of the city, and the Daughter Library in the precincts of the Temple of Serapis (*see* above), to house the book-rolls, said to number over 50,000, amassed on behalf of his father. Philadelpus never stinted money on buying yet more books for the Library of Alexandria.

In about 276 BC, Philadelphus married Arsinoe I, daughter of Lysimachus of Thrace and his queen, Nicaea, and added her possessions in the Aegean to Egypt's foreign territories. Lysimachus himself had taken a second wife, Philadelphus' sister, another Arsinoe, but in 281 BC Lysimachus and Seleucus of Babylon finally managed to kill each other in battle, leaving Arsinoe II a widow in a land far from home. She returned to Egypt, and was soon embroiled in jealous rivalry with her step-daughter, her brother's queen. Arsinoe II accused her sister-in-law of treason and she was banished to Coptos in Upper Egypt, leaving Arsinoe II to seize her opportunity. In what was a shocking departure from Macedonian or Greek custom, but acceptable practice in Egypt, she persuaded her brother, Philadelphus, to marry her. No children were born of this incestuous union.

Philadelphus was succeeded by the son borne to him by the Thracian princess, Arsinoe I (*see* above), Ptolemy III Euergetes I (246-221 BC). The marriage of Euergetes (The Beneficent God) to Berenice II, daughter of Magas of Cyrene, united Cyrene with Egypt; and successful campaigns in Syria added to Egypt's foreign possessions. Euergetes I was not only a great general but a scholar. Like his father and grandfather he brought books to Alexandria, sometimes by ruthless methods. During a famine, he refused to sell grain to Athens unless the city agreed to send its copies of the works of Sophocles, Aeschylus and Euripides to be copied in Alexandria. Athens was forced to agree and the books were duly copied — but Euergetes I then sent the copies back to Athens and kept the originals in Alexandria. His reign, although marred by a terrible famine in Egypt itself, marked the peak of Ptolemaic power at home and expansion abroad. With the exception of one ruler, Cleopatra VII, his successors were weak and corrupt, indulging in family feuds and jealousies. Their incessant civil wars progressively impoverished Egypt, leaving the country weak and, by 80 BC, prey to the emerging power, Rome.

Egypt's Ptolemaic rulers never identified themselves with their Egyptian subjects, remaining Greek in language, culture and outlook, although at least they made no attempt to change the traditional way of life of the Egyptians. Their main preoccupation was rivalry, always domestic and often foreign, at first with other satraps and former satraps and later with their descendants, with enmity between Egypt and Syria taking pride of place. By the reign of Ptolemy III it was clear that a secure and well-financed base was needed for the successful prosecution of foreign wars; and that this could only be achieved with the cooperation of the Egyptians.

The Greek populace of Egypt despised the Egyptians and were scornful of what they considered to be their peculiar customs. They even mocked the Egyptian gods though Greeks were normally tolerant of other people's religions. In return, Egyptians hated the Greeks, often referring to them as 'Ionian dogs'; and the most passionate haters were the priests, who considered it their duty to protect the Egyptian way of life and customs from the 'Ionian dogs' and to continue their age-old role as repositories of knowledge. Gradually, however, the Ptolemaic kings came to a *modus vivendi* with the powerful priesthood: in return for its cooperation in the efficient administration of Egypt they, the Ptolemies, agreed to be treated like Egyptian kings, to adopt the royal regalia and titles, to have their names written in *cartouches*, to make offerings to the Egyptian gods, and above all, to pay for the building of new temples.

Temples in ancient Egypt played an important part in the life of the community, not as centres of worship for ordinary men and women, who were denied entrance to them, but as 'theatres' in which the religion of the state was enacted by its initiates, and as great bureaucratic centres. Temples owned land which was rented out to tenants, their priests ran the schools in which scribes, artists and doctors were trained. Doctor-priests were based in the temples from which they tended the sick; and some temples even had rudimentary hospitals. All kinds of legal document, from marriage contracts to law suits to records of birth and death, were drawn up by temple scribes and kept in temple archives. In a land where most of the population was illiterate, the temple scribe was a necessity, for he, like

1   Temple of Isis at Philae

the doctor-priests, was available to those who otherwise would not be able to afford such services.

The Ptolemies probably needed little persuasion that temples were necessary for the efficient running of the country; but they are unlikely to have realized that in allowing the priests to build new edifices they were providing them with the opportunity to demonstrate Egyptian nationalism. The new temples were not slavishly modelled on old Egyptian architectural forms, with some innovations, such as screen walls (*see* p. 67) and new, more elaborate, decorations on column capitals, being introduced; but the inscriptions on their walls, often carved in hieroglyphs intentionally made more elaborate and confusing than was normal, sometimes contained veiled insults to the Greeks. It must have given the priests great satisfaction to use the word *Mdy*, for example. *Mdy* was an epithet of the god Seth; but it could also mean Mede, as in Medes and Persians. Originally, the term referred to Persians, but by Ptolemaic times it meant enemies in general, and the Egyptians' Greek overlords in particular. Thus whenever priests chanted imprecations against *Mdy* while stabbing him with a knife or piercing him with a spear, they were with impunity symbolically killing Greeks.

It was probably no accident that four of the five major temples built in the Ptolemaic period are in Upper Egypt, relatively neglected by the Ptolemies because it was far away from Alexandria and not as economically useful to them as the more fertile Lower Egypt and the Delta. The inhabitants of Upper Egypt, and in particular, the Thebaïd, the area around modern-day Luxor, had a tendency to rebel: for some twenty years control of the Thebaïd was lost (*see* Glossary), and it was as late as 85 BC that the most serious revolt was put down. The fifth major temple of the period is just south of Egypt's southern border at Philae (**1**), reputedly the burial place of the left leg of Osiris, which the Egyptians considered to be the mythological source of the Nile. Philae was thus a religiously important site, even though it was situated in Nubia, a land not always under Egyptian control.

Edfu was the first new temple to be commissioned in the Ptolemaic era. Work on the nucleus of the building was begun in 237 BC, under Ptolemy III, and continued into the the reign of his successor, Ptolemy IV Philopator (221-205 BC). Philopator (The Father-loving God) also favoured Philae with his attention, initiating work on a chapel dedicated to Imhotep (*see* p. 46) which was to be finished by his successor. Philopator was forced to defend Palestine against the incursions of Antiochus III of Syria, and in 217 BC defeated him decisively at the Battle of Raphia in which, for the first time, native Egyptian troops served in the Ptolemaic army. The Egyptians claimed much credit for the victory and their resentment at a perceived lack of appreciation fuelled their nationalism, sparking off the first of a long series of revolts in Upper Egypt. In spite of this, the nucleus of Edfu Temple was completed in 212 BC; but in 208 BC Philopator lost control of the Thebaïd, most of which was annexed by Nubian kings. Naturally, work on Edfu Temple ceased.

It was not until the nineteenth year of the reign of Ptolemy V Epiphanes (205-180 BC) that the Thebaïd was brought back under control. Epiphanes (God-made-manifest) has a greater claim to fame, however. Several years after he came to the throne he was crowned according to Egyptian rites; and in 196 BC, in honour of this event, the Rosetta Stone, the most important key to the decipherment of hieroglyphs, was issued. During the reign of Epiphanes most of Egypt's foreign possessions were lost to the Seleucids and Macedonians; and his successors were too wrapped up in family rivalries to restore them. Epiphanes seems to have taken little interest in Edfu Temple; but in his reign a temple was begun at Kom Ombo (**colour plate 2**) dedicated, unusually, to two deities, Horus the Elder and Sobek, or Suchos, the crocodile god (**colour plate 3**). It was destined to take over twice as long to build as Edfu — its courtyard was completed in the reign of the Roman Emperor, Tiberius (AD 14-37), and the final decoration put into place under Macrinus (AD 217-218).

When Epiphanes died, his wife, Cleopatra I, daughter of Antiochus III of Syria, was left to act as regent for their son, Ptolemy VI Philometor (180-145 BC), a minor. Philometor (The Mother-loving God) lived up to his name by commissioning building work at Philae in the temple dedicated to the great mother-goddess, Isis. Cleopatra I was a capable ruler who made a determined effort to erode the barriers between her Greek and Egyptian subjects. She encouraged them to work together, and, outwith Alexandria at least, many Greeks married Egyptians and took up an Egyptian way of life. After the death of Cleopatra I in 176 BC, Philometor married his sister Cleopatra II; and in 170 BC,

2   *Temple of Khnum at Esna*

after invasion attempts by Antiochus IV of Syria, established joint rule with Cleopatra II and their brother, Euergetes II. Six years later he was ousted by Euergetes II, but returned the following year and, in spite of his brother's efforts, ruled with Cleopatra II until his death in 145 BC. Their son, Neos Philopator, was nominally king until 144 BC when Euergetes II had him murdered.

The new king, Ptolemy VIII Euergetes II (170-116 BC), consolidated his own hold on the throne immediately by marrying Cleopatra II. Their honeymoon was spent on a visit to Thebes (modern Luxor) and a tour of inspection of the nucleus of the temple at Edfu, which awaited completion. Two years later, the happy couple were present at its dedication. During the reign of Euergetes II, Edfu Temple was extended by the addition of a large columned hall, which was begun in 140 BC and completed sixteen years later. Euergetes II took an interest in other temples: in the temple at Esna (**2**) dedicated to the ram-headed god, Khnum, which had been founded during the reign of his brother, Philometor, and in the temple at Kom Ombo begun in the reign of his father, Ptolemy V Epiphanes. For the Temple of Isis at Philae, he commissioned a great pylon or monumental gateway.

Two years after his marriage to Cleopatra II, the king's eye fell upon her daughter; and Cleopatra III, no less ambitious than her mother, was willing to marry her uncle who was by then a repulsive figure known to the Alexandrians as

'Physkon' (Pot-belly). It was not a marriage in name only — she was to bear him five children. And so, between 143 BC and 101 BC, Euergetes II ruled Egypt with the two Cleopatras. In 132 BC, there was another revolt in the Thebaïd which was put down with great severity, with the inhabitants of Hermonthis (Armant) and several other cities being put to the sword. After a revolt in Alexandria, Euergetes II went into exile in Cyprus, taking with him Cleopatra III, their children and Memphites, his son by Cleopatra II. When Cleopatra II claimed sole possession of the throne, Euergetes II had their son, Memphites, put to death, and sent the child's dismembered body back to his mother.[2] Despite this, when Euergetes II returned to Egypt in 127 BC, Cleopatra II consented to rule alongside him and Cleopatra III.

In 116 BC, Ptolemy IX Soter II (known as Lathyros or 'Chickpea'), the eldest son of Euergetes II and Cleopatra III, came to the throne. He was a man of about twenty-five years of age, but his reign, and later that of his younger brother, Ptolemy X Alexander I (110-101 BC), was bedevilled by the hatreds and ambitions of their mother, Cleopatra III. On the death of Euergetes II, Soter II was elected joint ruler with his mother: she, however, preferred his more pliable brother, Alexander, and, after several unsuccessful attempts, managed to drive Soter II into exile. During his exile, Egypt was ruled by Ptolemy Alexander I, first with Cleopatra III, who died in 101 BC, and after her death with his niece, Cleopatra Berenice, daughter of Soter II. In 88 BC Ptolemy Alexander I died in a naval battle. Soter II regained the throne and for the next seven years ruled jointly with his daughter, Cleopatra Berenice.

In 88 BC, revolt broke out in the Thebaïd once again and three years later Thebes (Luxor) was destroyed. In spite of, or perhaps because of, the turbulence of Soter II's reign, work on the building of temples carried on vigorously. The decoration of the columned hall at Edfu begun in the reign of Euergetes II was carried out between 116 and 108 BC; and in 116 BC Soter II ordered the construction of a forecourt, a pylon gateway (*see* Glossary) and an enclosure wall to surround the whole temple. At the same time, the building of the great Temple of Hathor at Denderah (**3**) was begun.

In 80 BC, Soter II was succeeded by his nephew, Ptolemy XI Alexander II, son of Ptolemy X. His reign lasted for less than a year: having married and, nineteen days later, killed Cleopatra Berenice, he was murdered by an Alexandrian mob. The last legitimate male member of the Ptolemaic dynasty, he was succeeded by an illegitimate son of Soter II. The new king was Ptolemy XII Neos Dionysos (80-51 BC), nicknamed Auletes or 'the flute player', who reigned as a king whose hold on the throne of Egypt depended upon the patronage of Rome. Like his predecessors, he found it politic to cultivate the Egyptian priesthood, and in his reign a great columned hall was built at Kom Ombo, and a pylon gateway begun at Philae. At Edfu, the decoration of the forecourt, pylon gateway and enclosure wall begun in the reign of Soter II was unfinished; nevertheless, in 71 BC, Auletes performed their dedication ceremony.

In 58 BC, Auletes was forced into exile in Rome. In his absence, the Temple of

3   Temple of Hathor at Denderah

Edfu was finally finished when, in 57 BC, the great doors of its pylon gateway were hung — two years before Julius Caesar invaded Britain. Auletes was restored three years later by Gabinius, but in 51 BC he died and was succeeded by his son, Ptolemy XIII, a twelve-year-old boy. Ptolemy XIII married his sister, Cleopatra VII and ruled jointly with her but soon expelled her. In 48 BC he was forced by Caesar to take her back, whereupon he joined a revolt against Caesar during which he drowned in the Nile. In his short reign, however, Ptolemy XIII had finished the pylon gateway at Philae started in the reign of his father; and commissioned the building of a second pylon gateway there.

Cleopatra VII married her younger brother, another twelve year old called Ptolemy. When Cleopatra followed Caesar to Rome, Ptolemy XIV remained in Egypt to rule alone, but was poisoned by Cleopatra when she returned to Egypt in 44 BC after the death of Caesar. In 47 BC Cleopatra had given birth to Caesar's son, Caesarion; and it is he who is depicted with his mother in the famous relief on the exterior wall of the Temple of Hathor at Denderah (**4**). Cleopatra, the greatest of the Ptolemies, the only one of the dynasty who spoke Egyptian, was possibly the most ambitious of them all. She was intelligent and highly capable, charming when it suited her, seducing people, especially men, not with the beauty of her face, for apparently this was not classically beautiful, but with the beauty of her voice, willing to use her body to gain her political ends. Having lost Caesar she made an alliance with his protégé, Antony, by whom she had three children. Caesarion shared the throne of Egypt with his mother; but the ambition of Antony and Cleopatra was to set up his siblings on thrones of their own. Their

4   *Cleopatra and Caesarion: relief on rear wall at Denderah*

attempts to establish an empire in the east inevitably brought them into conflict with Rome; and in 30 BC, Antony and Cleopatra's defeat at the hands of Caesar's nephew, Octavianus, brought the Ptolemaic Dynasty to an end.

2 The Mythology of Horus

Many gods in ancient Egypt were worshipped in the form of falcons: major deities such as the sun god, Re, who took shape as a hawk-headed man wearing the sun's disk on his head; the war god, Montu, another hawk-headed man; and Sokar, a god of the Underworld who was represented as a mummified falcon, and lesser gods such as Anty, 'The Clawed One', and Dwn-antwy, 'He-of-the-Outstretched-Talons'. At Sekhem (Greek: Letopolis, modern Ausim), capital of the Second District of Lower Egypt, a falcon-god was worshipped as Mekhentenirty or 'The Face-which-is-without-Eyes', a sightless god whose original manifestation was as a shrew-mouse, commonly thought to be blind. Mekhentenirty's blindness caused him to be identified with Horus who was himself, according to myth, temporarily blinded by his enemy, Seth (*see* p. 33).

Horus was originally a sky-god worshipped in the form of a falcon (**colour plate 1**). The oldest Horus was a deity whose two eyes were the sun and the moon, although sometimes Horus became the sun itself, worshipped under the name Re-Horakhty, or Re-and-Horus-of-the-Two-Horizons. There were many forms of Horus, some more important than others, and the myths associated with them became intertwined making the mythology very complicated. One aspect of Horus was probably inspired by actual events dating back to prehistoric, predynastic, times, that is, before 3100 BC. Originally, Horus seems to have been a Lower Egyptian or northern deity, matched in the south or Upper Egypt by the god Seth; but his followers displaced the cult of Seth and from then on Horus became an Upper Egyptian god. In due course, the clans of Upper Egypt, united under the rule of one king and adherents of Horus, conquered Lower Egypt, and around 3100 BC the First Dynasty of Kings of Upper and Lower Egypt was founded.

The duality of Egypt was never forgotten throughout the course of ancient Egyptian history, and was reflected in two of the five names in the royal titulary: the Two Ladies Name, the ladies being Wadjet, the cobra-goddess who protected Lower Egypt, and Nekhbet, the vulture-goddess who protected Upper Egypt; and the name that actually states that the King ruled over the two halves of the land, the *nsw-bit* or King of Upper and Lower Egypt. Two of the other names in the royal titulary, the Horus and the Golden Horus, identify the King with the god who was regarded as his protector; and the fifth name, Son of Re, links the King with Re, who in some of his aspects was a manifestation of Horus. Every King of

Egypt was regarded as the living Horus, and the throne was called 'The Seat of Horus'.

The most famous Horus belonged to the mythology connected with *Iunu* or 'Pillar-city', usually known by the Greek name Heliopolis (City-of-the-Sun). The priesthood of *Iunu* claimed that the world was created by the sun-god, Re. He brought into existence Shu, god of air, and Tefnut, goddess of moisture, and they in turn brought into existence Geb, the earth god, and Nut, the sky goddess. Geb and Nut became the parents of Osiris, Isis, Horus the Elder, Seth and Nephthys. Osiris married his sister, Isis, and Seth became the husband of Nephthys, and they, together with their parents and grandparents and their brother Horus the Elder became the Ennead of Heliopolis, the group of nine deities who made up the family of Re.

Eventually, Re appointed Osiris King of Egypt, and for thirty-three years Osiris ruled Egypt wisely and well. When he decided to journey abroad in order to bring the arts of civilization to the rest of the world, he left Isis behind as Regent. Seth, who was already envious of Osiris' marriage to Isis, was resentful because he thought that he should have been named Regent, and when Osiris returned to Egypt laden with the praises of the countries he had visited, Seth became unbearably jealous. He invited Osiris to a party during which Osiris was trapped inside a great wooden chest which Seth cast into the Nile. The chest was swept down the river and into the Mediterranean where it floated eastwards until it reached Byblos in the Lebanon. There it was washed up on the shore and soon a great tamarisk tree had grown up round it, enclosing the chest and its divine contents within its trunk. The King of Byblos cut down the tree and made it into the main pillar in the great hall of his palace.

Meantime, Isis was seeking her husband; and after a long search found herself in Byblos, where, incognito, she became nursemaid to the King's infant son. He was ailing and the goddess, who was as great a magician as Re himself, began the process of curing him. Every night, when the palace was quiet, she set the child in a ring of fire until, one night, the queen, curious to find out why her son's health was improving, crept along to the nursery. Just as she reached it, the nursemaid emerged and made her way towards the great hall. The queen followed her and saw her change herself into a swallow which flew round and round the main pillar in the hall, making mournful sounds. The queen stood astonished for a time and then rushed back to the nursery to see whether this nursemaid-magician had harmed her son. When she saw him engulfed in flames she shrieked so loudly that her husband and his retainers came running to find out what was happening. Once the King had realized that the nursemaid was a goddess, he lost no time in begging her pardon; and Isis graciously accepted the pillar in the main hall of the palace as a propitiatory gift.

Isis retrieved the chest containing her husband's body from the tree trunk and sailed with it back to Egypt. There she set the body down on the shore and left it while she went to find Re to see what could be done. While she was away, Seth came across the body of Osiris; and this time he was determined that Isis should never find it again. He cut it up into pieces and strewed them throughout the length and breadth of Egypt. When Isis returned she was distraught; but, aided by her sister, Nephthys, she eventually collected together the pieces of her husband's body, all except his penis, which had been swallowed by a fish (*see* p. 77). This, however, did not prevent the resourceful goddess from becoming pregnant; and while Osiris was resurrected to become chief deity of the Underworld, Isis made her way to Chemmis in the Delta to await the birth of her son, Horus, who would, she was determined, one day succeed his father as King of Egypt. When Horus was fifteen, his mother took him before the tribunal of the gods to claim his inheritance. It was to be eighty years before he finally overcame his rival, Seth, but eventually Horus became King of Egypt.

During one of Horus' encounters with Seth, he was discovered by his enemy aleep on a mountain-side. Seth straddled Horus and gouged out his eyes, which he then planted in the ground. Horus' eyes were restored to him by the goddess Hathor and the healed eye of Horus, the *wadjet*-eye, became one of the most potent symbols in Egyptian mythology. Hathor herself, who was in one of her many forms a sky goddess whose name means 'House-of-Horus', was sometimes viewed, like Isis, as the mother of Horus. Another of her aspects was that of the fierce lioness that Re sent to destroy mankind; but the Greeks equated her with Aphrodite, goddess of love, and it is this Hathor, not only goddess of love, but also of happiness, dancing and music, who was worshipped in her great temple at Denderah; and it was Hathor of Denderah who became the wife of Horus.

At Edfu, Horus was worshipped as a falcon called Horus of Behdet. The mythology of Horus of Behdet seems to have been based upon the story of a warrior king of Lower Egypt whose battles were fought against the Seth-worshipping kings of Upper Egypt. Eventually the legends concerning these battles became solarized, so that Horus of Behdet, in destroying his own enemies, destroyed those of the sun god Re. Finally, the legends were Osirianized, and Horus of Behdet became identified with Horus son of Isis and Osiris, who replaced Horus the Elder in the Ennead of Heliopolis. Horus the Elder had helped Isis bury Osiris, but once the myth had become Osirianized it was Horus son of Isis who was said to have performed this task. His action influenced the way in which a king claimed the throne, which was by burying his predecessor just as Horus had buried the old King of Egypt, his father, Osiris.

In the mythology of Horus, the god is perpetually seeking to take revenge upon Seth, the murderer of his father, and the eternal struggle between Horus and Seth came to be regarded as a conflict that maintained the preservation of the essential balance of forces in the universe.

3 Egyptian Temples and their Decoration

There were two types of temple in Egypt, the cult and the memorial. The former was devoted to the worship of a god, or sometimes of several deities, and was the house in which the god lived, as the ancient Egyptian term — *pr nt̠r*, 'the house (*pr*) of the god (*nt̠r*)' — indicates. The latter was devoted to the worship of a dead king. At first, temples were constructed of reed and mud; later, sun-dried mud-brick was used. A lattice-work shrine seems to have been the earliest form of religious building in Egypt but, not surprisingly, no actual examples have survived. The oldest representation of such a hut-shrine dates to the reign of the First-Dynasty king, Aha (*c.* 3000 BC) and is carved on the wooden label from an oil jar found at Abydos.[1] Amongst other things, the label records the building of a sanctuary at Sais dedicated to the goddess Neit. The shrine depicted on the label consists of a courtyard enclosed by a lattice-work fence. At one end of the courtyard is a gateway with two masts flying flags; at the opposite end a hut-shrine, before which stands the emblem of Neit.

By the Third Dynasty (*c.* 2800 BC) the Egyptians were building in stone. The oldest stone-built temples were those attached to pyramids as memorial temples, the earliest being that belonging to the Step Pyramid at Sakkara (*see* p. 46). The cult temples of the earliest periods of Egyptian history have largely disappeared, thanks chiefly to the Egyptian custom of building new temples on sites that, as they put it, had been used 'since the time of the gods', in other words, since time immemorial, so that new structures obliterated the old. However, many temples of the Eighteenth Dynasty onwards (from about 1500 BC), both cult and memorial, still stand; and the cult temples of the Ptolemaic period in particular demonstrate that those who constructed in stone never forgot the early shrines built of reeds and mud. Thus they commemorated the original reed shrines in the basic decoration of each temple,[2] which was a copy in stone of the building methods and materials used in the wood and reed originals.

Two forms characteristic of Egyptian architecture, seen to best advantage in temples of the Ptolemaic period, are derived from the materials and methods used in the construction of the original reed shrines. The walls of these shrines, which were made from interwoven palm-sticks or reeds covered with a thick coating of mud, needed strengthening. This was done by binding together bundles of reeds or palm-sticks and lashing them to the corners of the walls, a practice still evident today in the reed shelters Egyptian peasants sometimes construct. Translated into stone, these reinforcements became the *torus* roll **(colour plate 4)**, the decorative rounded moulding found at the edges of walls. Reed or palm walls were also reinforced with a binding a foot or two below the top, leaving the reeds and palm fronds above the binding unsupported and liable to bend over. The curved effect this produced was imitated in the *cavetto* cornice **(colour plate 4)** found in stone temples.

Stone columns were copies of the supports made from tree trunks or bundles of plant-stems that were used in the earliest buildings. Accordingly, stone columns often have five bands carved below the capital, imitating the thongs with which the bunches of stems in the original forms were held together. Many of the plants used to make early forms of column must sometimes have flowered despite no longer being planted in the ground; and it is probably this flowering that inspired some of the decoration of the capitals of stone columns. The varieties of capital employed reflect their vegetable origin, being carved to represent palm-fronds, lotus buds and papyrus umbels; and in the Ptolemaic and Roman periods, especially, the campaniform capital, a composite derived from many varieties of flower, real and imaginary, was popular.

The monumental gateway to a temple consisted of two massive stone towers, or wings, each broader at the base than at the top, connected by a bridge over a central doorway and fronted by tall wooden masts, often higher than the towers and topped with pennants that floated in the breeze. The origin of this type of gateway, which is called a pylon and was not a feature of Egyptian architecture until about 1500 BC, lay in the towers of mud and woven reeds that stood outside primitive reed shrines. The decoration of pylon gateways, like that of temple walls, reproduced in stone the features of reed architecture; thus they have *cavetto* cornices and *torus* roll edgings.

The decoration of a cult temple in particular is also a reflection of the mythological origins of the world and the creation of the first shrine. An explanation of how the world began was an important element in ancient Egyptian religion, with each major centre of worship having its own variant of a creation legend. The Egyptians' own experience of living in a country that was covered annually by the flood water of the Nile from which, as it receded, land first reappeared in the form of muddy mounds, provided them with the imagery to describe the creation of the world. All the creation legends agreed on one thing: that before the world began, only a vast sheet of water existed in a dark infinity of nothingness called Chaos. This primeval sea was personified as Nun.

At Heliopolis, it was said that the oldest sun-god, Atum, having brought himself into existence, floated in the watery Nun until, becoming lonely, he engendered two children to keep him company but became separated from them. After a long, frantic search in the immense stretch of water, Atum found his lost children, for whom he then created a mound in the primeval waters so that they might live safely on dry land. It was this mound that was represented as the *benben*, the pyramid-shaped stone that was worshipped in the temples of the sun-gods Atum and Re. Other creation legends claimed that the primordial mound

5   North Enclosure Wall, Edfu Temple: the Creation Legend of Horus of Behdet

emerged from the waters of the Nun in the form of the god Ta-tjenen, whose name means 'The land (*Ta*) which has risen (*tjenen*)', the inference being that it had arisen out of Nun. At Esna, it was said that the primeval, asexual, goddess, Neit, rested on the mound to give birth to the sun, thus bringing about the beginning of the world. At Hermopolis, there was a tradition that the local god, Thoth, placed on the sacred mound an egg from which the young sun emerged to rise up into the sky. Another tradition at Hermopolis described the birth of the sun in a different way. In this version, a lotus appeared on the dark water of the primeval sea, its petals closed. Eventually, a light enclosed by the petals became so brilliant that it forced the petals to open, revealing the infant sun, who spread his rays over the primeval sea, thus creating the first dawn.

At Edfu, inscriptions on the interior of the temple's Enclosure Wall[3] (**5**) describe how, before the world began, Chaos reigned until, out of Chaos, a mound emerged that was wreathed in darkness and surrounded by the primeval waters. Two amorphous beings, the Great One and the Distant One, emerged from the waters and pulled up a reed growing at the edge of the mound, which the inscriptions name the Island of Trampling. Having split the reed in two, they

37

stuck one half into the ground; and at once, a falcon appeared and alighted upon the perch formed from the split reed. Light broke over Chaos. A simple reed shelter was constructed around the falcon sitting on his perch to afford him some protection; and he was acclaimed as the Divine Falcon by the Great One and the Distant One, who became the ancestral deities of Edfu Temple, worshipped as the *Shebtiw*.[4] According to inscriptions at Edfu Temple, as the waters of the primeval sea receded, rooms were added on to the original hut until finally the first temple came into being.

The mythological origin of the temple is reflected in architectural features that are found in buildings of both the Pharaonic and Ptolemaic periods. The stone columns of a temple represented in re-grouped order the reeds that grew round the primeval island. Thus, the bases of these columns were often engraved with marsh plants. In the memorial temple of Ramesses III (1184-1153 BC) at Medinet Habu, for example, and in all the Ptolemaic temples, there is a slight but distinct rise in floor level from the outer hall of the temple through to the Sanctuary, in commemoration of the fact that the first, mythological, sanctuary was erected at the highest point on the Island of Creation. Each temple precinct was surrounded by a high mud-brick wall, the *temenos* wall. In cult temples of the Pharaonic and Ptolemaic periods, such as those at Karnak and Denderah respectively, and at memorial temples such as Medinet Habu, it can clearly be seen that this wall is built in alternately concave and convex sections, giving an impression of wavy lines. There seems to be no architectural purpose for building in such a way, and the conclusion must be that this method of constructing a *temenos* wall is an attempt to represent the waves of the primeval ocean that surrounded the Island of Creation.

Mythology accounted for certain other features of the temples of the Graeco-Roman period, namely the special buildings that were erected for the annual celebration of the birth of the god of the temple, or, in the case of Denderah, the place where the goddess, Hathor, gave birth to her son. These buildings, known today as *mammisi* or 'Birth Houses', developed from the practice, during the Pharaonic period, of recording the theogamy ritual (*see* p. 19) in temples, most famously in a colonnade in the memorial temple of Hatshepsut (1479-1457 BC) at Deir el-Bahri, where a set of reliefs records the Queen's divine conception and birth, and in a small chapel in Luxor Temple, in which the inscriptions recording the divine birth of Amenhotep III (1383-1345 BC) are copied almost verbatim from Hatshepsut's version. By the Ptolemaic period such chapels had developed into independent structures, set usually in front of the temple and at right angles to it. From the time of Ptolemy VI onwards a typical *mammisi* consisted of a rectangular sanctuary fronted by a square hall for the presentation of offerings. A columned corridor ran round the sides and rear of the sanctuary but was separated from a columned vestibule at the front by two doorways. A *mammisi* was intended to be an architectural representation of the papyrus thicket in which Isis gave birth to Horus. Thus, the columns of the corridor represented the papyrus plants in the thicket; and their papyriform capitals punned on the word *w3ḏ*, which in ancient

Egyptian meant not only papyrus and papyriform but also green, young and infant.

If each temple was a reproduction of the landscape of the primeval Island of Creation, it was also a reflection of the physical world as a whole — the sky, the earth, the natural features and the vegetable forms found on earth.[5] The floor of a temple was paved in plain undecorated stone; nevertheless, it represented the earth out of which plants grew. Thus the dado at the base of a wall was often carved with lily or lotus plants, and with lines of human figures proceeding along the dado as the personified forms of the canals, fields and districts of Egypt, all bearing their produce, and above all, of the Nile, Hapy. The ceilings in a temple were often painted blue studded with gold-coloured stars to represent the sky. Pylon gateways also played a role in the interpretation of the temple as a reflection of the physical world, with their two wings representing the hills of the horizon behind which the sun rises and sets. At Edfu, the east wing of the Pylon gateway was identified with Manu, the mythical mountain said to lie on the eastern horizon, and the west wing with Bakhau, the mythical mountain on the western horizon.[6]

It is difficult to see that primitive shrines could have had any elaborate mythical interpretation of their significance; and it is clear that the basic decoration of stone-built temples, where it is derived from natural or vegetable forms, or from primitive building methods and materials, must have occurred spontaneously. Nevertheless, it is equally clear that the various elements of a stone-built temple were constructed according to architectural conventions that symbolized the mythological origin of the temple, and in addition lent themselves to a more complex theory of the cosmological significance of the temple's decoration. Each temple represented the earthly home of one or more gods and was constructed so as to resemble the sky in which they normally dwelt. The Egyptians believed that the sky rested upon mountains set at the four corners of the earth, and that it was divided into four regions. Thus the temple's four cardinal points represented the celestial regions and its columns were compared to the mountains which held up the sky. The rooms on the left side of a temple were equated with the eastern half of the sky, and those on the right side corresponded to the western half.

Like the universe, a temple was a mystical theatre in which were enacted the great events pertaining to Egypt. It was not a theatre open to the public, however. The temple as a whole could be divided into public, private and sacred sections. On certain occasions privileged people were allowed through the pylon gateway of a temple into the forecourt, which can thus be termed the private section. Only the king and priests could enter the sacred section, that is, those areas of the temple which lay beyond the forecourt as far as the sanctuary. The ordinary man or woman was not normally allowed to enter the main body of a temple, and the exterior of the enclosure wall and pylon gateway was all that could be seen by the general public. It was the exterior walls of a temple, therefore, that were chosen by its builders as suitable places on which to place dedicatory inscriptions (*see* p. 51) celebrating the circumstances in which the temple was built, almost as though

6   Roof, Edfu Temple: dummy door with opening at bottom for water-spout

these inscriptions were public announcements.

Certain architectural features indicate that the exterior of a temple was concerned with the protection of Egypt. At Denderah and Edfu, for example, the exterior of the *Naos* or nucleus of the temple is decorated with lion-headed gargoyles which house water-spouts intended to remove water from the temple roof. Rain rarely occurred, and the water must, therefore, have been that used in ceremonies performed on the roof. In the parapet that runs round the roof of each temple are carved dummy doors (**6**) with holes at the bottom leading into the water-spouts housed in the gargoyles. This water was not in its original usage deemed harmful; but in sweeping it from the temple roof the priests turned it into a symbol of evil. Thus, in spitting out the water, the gargoyles symbolically spat out evil away from Egypt, as personified by the temple.

The public sections of a temple were used as showcases for depicting the triumph of Egypt over its enemies. Pylon gateways were decorated with scenes of gods and kings, sculpted on heroic scale, killing or taking captive enemies. In this way, not only was Egypt's triumph symbolized and its continuation magically ensured, but the Egyptians could behold their king in his victory and be heartened by it. A temple was thought to represent Egypt itself; hence scenes of war carved on its exterior walls were thought to give protection, by magical means, to the country. Many such scenes demonstrate a purposeful orientation, being carved on walls facing the directions in which enemy countries lay. Thus in the Temple of Amun at Karnak scenes depicting the Asiatic wars of Sety I (1294-1279 BC) are found on the exterior of the north wall of the Hypostyle Hall — correct geographically, since the Asiatics came from lands to the north-east of Egypt. At Medinet Habu, the exterior of the north wall of the temple depicts the battles of Ramesses III (1184-1153 BC) against the Sea Peoples, an attack which came from the north; but his battles against the Libyans, who came from the west, are found on the west wall of the temple. In Graeco-Roman temples, even a *mammisi* follows this geographical discipline. The scene depicting Isis suckling the infant Horus is usually found on the rear wall of the sanctuary. At Denderah, Kom Ombo and Philae, the rear wall of the sanctuary is the north wall; at Edfu, it is the south wall. In terms of local orientation, taking into account the direction of the flow of the Nile, the rear walls of all these sanctuaries are oriented purposefully towards Chemmis in the northern Delta where lay the papyrus thicket in which Isis suckled her child (*see* p. 33).

A temple was also the setting for the celebration of rites and ceremonies designed to ensure the well-being of the king and his people. The basic decoration of a temple, together with certain architectural features, formed the framework for a more particular decoration in which the all-important rites and ceremonies were recorded in the form of reliefs and inscriptions sculpted upon the walls of the temple, the underlying principle of which was to ensure, by magical processes, the security and success of Egypt throughout eternity. That such representations had potency was a longstanding belief of the ancient Egyptians, who made sure that the dead were everlastingly equipped with provisions by depicting them upon the walls of tombs, and with servants by placing in the tombs models and statuettes which were intended to come to life in the Afterworld for the benefit of the deceased. Such was the intensity of belief that figures in reliefs had the capacity to come alive and perhaps do harm that they were often mutilated to prevent them doing so. Even in inscriptions scribes sometimes depicted potentially dangerous animals, reptiles or human beings, represented in the hieroglyphs, cut in two or transfixed with daggers to render them impotent.[7]

Even temples of the Pharaonic period sometimes had recorded upon their walls a summary of the rituals that were enacted before them, such summaries acting as *aides mémoire* for the priestly officiants. In Ptolemaic temples it is clear that ceremonies and rituals were not carved on the walls in a haphazard way, and that a relief, or more especially a text, would not have been placed upon a wall if its presence in that particular place did not have a significance and a precise role to play. Obviously, not all reliefs may be taken as depicting the literal truth: it is not possible, for instance, that the scenes of sacrifice that decorate the walls of the crypts in the Temple of Hathor at Denderah indicate that such scenes were enacted in the crypts themselves, which are too small. But the decoration of the rooms and halls within a temple was seldom meaningless.

As far as the Temple of Edfu is concerned, it is possible to draw up a series of 'rules' concerning the layout of scenes upon various walls of the temple. The reliefs on each wall are divided into rows, called registers, by horizontal lines which run beneath the feet of the sculpted figures. There are usually three registers, but there can be two or four depending on the height of the wall, and the reliefs and inscriptions on each are divided into scenes, which are either square or rectangular, and are separated by vertical lines of inscription running down their left and right sides. These vertical lines of inscription, which are found throughout the temple, conform to a pattern. The line behind the relief of the king ideally contains the following: 'Long live the good god', the son (or heir etc.), followed by epithets of the king, followed by 'The Lord of Appearances' and a *cartouche*. The line on the opposite side of the scene, behind the figure or figures of deities, contains a winged disk, divine epithets, and the god's name followed by more epithets.

The figure of a deity was sculpted in each scene facing in the direction that would ensure that he, or she, always had his face turned towards those who entered the temple, or a room within the temple. This was considered so important that a sculptor would sometimes even turn a hieroglyph depicting a god against the prevailing direction of the surrounding hieroglyphs so that the god faced towards the entrance of the room or temple.[8] In each room or hall the scenes normally are read from the entrance of the room, or hall, to the mid-point of the rear wall. This convention was based on the belief that the god occupied a place at the far end of the room facing towards the entrance: the ritual thus develops towards the god, with the reading beginning on the wall to the left of the door to the room, then crossing to the wall on its right. The same general rule applies to the reading of scenes in the temple overall: the sanctuary of the god being in the innermost part of the building it follows that the order of scenes develops from the outer door of the temple towards the interior. It should be noted, however, that there are exceptions to this rule (*see* p. 113); and that a ritual may progress from place to place within the temple.

Scenes are read register by register, normally from the bottom register to the top. The Egyptians considered that the bottom register told of events that happened nearest in time, the top register of events furthest away in time. The bottom register, therefore, normally concerns rites that were performed before those on the top register. Sometimes, as in the Daily Ritual (*see* p. 80), a ritual is made up of scenes on three registers of two walls, with those on the first register being read horizontally along the wall, alternately from left/west to right/east (*see* below), but those on the second and third registers being read upwards vertically in pairs. The walls of each room or hall in the temple are decorated with scenes depicting the ritual or rituals that were celebrated in it; and the development of each individual ritual governs the order in which the scenes within the ritual are to be read. This varies from room to room for there is no uniform order of reading scenes throughout the temple as a whole.

Because, around 3100 BC, Upper Egypt had conquered Lower Egypt to unite the two halves of Egypt, Upper Egypt always took precedence over the conquered land. Thus, scenes concerning Lower Egypt are read before those concerning Upper Egypt, on the principle that the most important person in a procession walks at the rear, preceded by less important persons in order of rank. Upper

Egyptian scenes are normally found on the right, or eastern walls, of Edfu Temple, Lower Egyptian scenes on the left or western walls. The King depicted performing the ritual wears the appropriate crowns — the White Crown of Upper Egypt in scenes on the eastern walls, the Red Crown of Lower Egypt on the western walls. This convention can sometimes appear to be broken (*see* p. 42), but close inspection of the development of a ritual sometimes proves that where the order of the ritual demands it, scenes may be read from the inside of the temple, or a room within the temple, to the outside. In such cases, the overriding 'rule' is that Lower Egyptian scenes are depicted on the left-hand wall, Upper Egyptian scenes on the right-hand wall, even when this results in left no longer being synonymous with west or right with east.

A ritual may be depicted upon one wall only; and when this happens, the wall is divided into two vertical halves, one for Upper Egypt, the other for Lower Egypt. The scenes making up the ritual may then be divided between Upper and Lower Egypt and allotted to the appropriate half of the wall — normally the left half for Lower Egypt, the right for Upper Egypt. When a wall is divided in this way, the order of reading the ritual begins with the outermost Lower-Egyptian scene, moves across to the outermost Upper-Egyptian scene, and so on, reading inwards alternately left to right until the midpoint of the wall is reached. A ritual may be depicted on only one register, the rest of the wall being devoted to other rituals; and occasionally lack of space meant that scenes were not drawn up in parallel, with separate sets for Upper and Lower Egypt.

It is clear that at Edfu and other temples the reliefs and inscriptions on the exterior walls and on the walls of inner rooms and halls had a magical purpose. The decoration of the temple interior was never haphazard but a deliberate attempt to record the rituals once performed there. Thus the walls of its inner rooms and chapels can be regarded as source books in stone of the rites and liturgy enacted in the temple, where, it was claimed in an inscription on Edfu's Enclosure Wall, 'every ritual is in the place where it ought to be'.[9]

4 The Temple of Horus at Edfu

History of the Temple

The modern town of Edfu lies on the west bank of the Nile some 60 miles (100km) to the south of Luxor, half way between Luxor and Aswan. It was known to the ancient Egyptians as *Wetjeset-Hor* or 'The-Place-where-Horus-is-Extolled' and from an early date was the site of a shrine dedicated to the god, Horus (*see* map, p. 14). *Wetjeset-Hor* was an important and prosperous city, thanks largely to the fact that it was close to routes giving access to the gold mines in the Eastern Desert, notably along the Wadi Abbad which is only 15 miles (24km) to the east. It is thought that at the beginning of Egyptian history, *Wetjeset-Hor* was the chief city of an area that had its southern border at the First Cataract while its northern border was contiguous with the district later known as the Thebaïd (*see* Glossary), and that it was to all intents and purposes independent of the kings who ruled Egypt from Memphis, far away in the north. Eventually, however, it was absorbed into Egypt proper. The title 'Great Chief' of the district is first attested at *Wetjeset-Hor* at the beginning of the Sixth Dynasty, in the reign of King Teti (*c.* 2345-2333 BC); and one of the holders of the office, Isi, whose tomb is some 200m south-west of the town temple, was appointed vizier, one of the most important offices of state. By the end of the Dynasty, *Wetjeset-Hor* had become the capital of the Second District of Upper Egypt, to which it gave its name.

Evidence shows that a temple existed at *Wetjeset-Hor* throughout the historical period. The building had both a sacred and a secular name. The former was *Behdet*, which means 'seat' or 'throne', and seems to have been used first in the Third Dynasty when the local god Horus merged with the Horus of the Delta town, *Behdet*. From then on, the temple at *Wetjeset-Hor* was called *Behdet*; and its Horus became Horus of Behdet. The secular name for his temple was *Djeba*, which means 'Retribution Town', a reference to the fact that the enemies of the god were brought to justice there. The temple had several other appellations — *Mesen* (The-Place-of-the Harpoon), the Mansion of Re, *Nedjem-Ankh* (Pleasant-to-Live-In), the Window of the Falcon, the Shrine of Horus and *Wetjeset* (The-Place-of-Extolling-the-God). The Greeks identified Horus with the sun-god, Apollo, and called the town Apollinopolis Magna. By the Coptic era (*see* Glossary) the pronunciation of the word *Djeba* had become Etbo, which has become Edfu in Arabic, the language spoken in Egypt today. Thus the secular name for the Temple of Horus has become the name of the town in which it lies.

According to tradition, the first stone temple built at *Wetjeset-Hor* was designed by Imhotep, said to be the son of the great god of Memphis, Ptah, and a woman named Khredu-ankh. Imhotep, a real man who lived in the Third Dynasty (around 2660 BC), was a high official of King Djoser, for whose burial he is thought to have designed the great Step Pyramid at Sakkara. This is the earliest building in dressed stone in the world, making Imhotep the first named architect of stone buildings. Although his own tomb is as yet undiscovered, he is almost certainly buried at Sakkara. A statue base discovered near the entrance to the precinct of the Step Pyramid, with which it was probably contemporaneous, is inscribed with one of King Djoser's official names, and with Imhotep's name and titles. The titles give an indication of the man's versatility: 'Chancellor of the King of Upper and Lower Egypt, the first after the King of Upper Egypt, administrator of the Great Palace, hereditary noble, High Priest of Heliopolis, Imhotep, the builder, the sculptor.'

Imhotep was also a sage and a magician; and was traditionally supposed to have been the author of several books, although none of them has survived. He was regarded as the patron of scribes and statuettes typically show him as a shaven-headed man seated with a papyrus-roll spread open on his knees. It was the custom with scribes to sprinkle a few drops of water from their pots before they began work, in honour of Imhotep, the Sage, the Scribe. At Sakkara, a temple dedicated to Imhotep stood near the Serapeum, the catacombs where the sacred Apis bulls were buried, and during the so-called Late Period of Egyptian history (525-332 BC), when the Egyptians were driven by centuries of foreign occupation to look back into their own history for inspirational figures, Imhotep's temple became especially popular as a place of pilgrimage.

Imhotep's reputation as a god of healing brought sick people, especially cripples, from all over Egypt flocking to his temple at Sakkara, and to shrines dedicated to him at Karnak, Deir el-Bahri and Deir el-Medina. The Greeks called his temple at Sakkara the Asklepieion, an indication that they identified Imhotep, whom they called Imouthes, with their own great physician, Asklepios; and a chapel was built for Imhotep at Philae in the reigns of Ptolemy IV Philopator and Ptolemy V Epiphanes. It is not surprising, therefore, that the priests of Edfu Temple claimed that the first temple built of stone was constructed there in the Third Dynasty by the famous architect of the Step Pyramid, Imhotep, using a plan that, it was said, 'fell from heaven'. Figures of Imhotep appear in several places in the temple; but in the north-eastern corner of the outer wall of the Ambulatory (*see* p. 65), the inscription refers to 'The grand master of ceremonies, the great Imhotep, son of Ptah' and goes on to claim that the temple was constucted in accordance with the principles laid down by the master.

Little is known of the earliest temple at Edfu except that it was dedicated to Horus, Hathor of Denderah and *Hor-sma-tawy*, their son. In the Nineteenth Dynasty, Sety I (1294-1279 BC) and his son, Ramesses II (1279-1213), had work done on it, as did Ramesses III (1184-1153) in the following Dynasty (**7**); and the name of Ramesses III is inscribed in several places on the remains of the original

7 *Forecourt, Edfu Temple, AD 1984, dug up to reveal the remains of the earlier temple*

structure's pylon gateway, which lies outside the east wall of the present temple. The most significant piece of work to survive from the original building is the highly polished black syenite shrine, over 4m high, that was dedicated by King Nectanebo II (360-343 BC) of the Thirtieth Dynasty. The builders of the Ptolemaic temple obviously considered it fine enough to use in the Sanctuary of their new building, where it stands to this day.

By the Ptolemaic period, the temple refurbished by the Ramessides, which was probably comparatively small and suffering from years of neglect, was deemed inadequate for the needs of the busy capital of an important district, and was a prime candidate for the temple-building programme of Ptolemy III Euergetes I, who ordered a new, sandstone temple to be built, on a massive scale, on the site of the older structure. The new temple was dedicated to Horus of Behdet. Its nucleus, which is in itself a complete temple and consists of a sanctuary surrounded by seventeen cult chambers and store rooms, an eight-pillared hall, two smaller halls, and two staircases leading to the roof, was begun in 237 BC and finished twenty-five years later, although the decoration of its walls took a further six years. In 206 BC, work on the temple was brought to a halt by an insurrection in the Thebaïd in which two local potentates declared themselves independent of Ptolemaic rule. It was to be twenty years before the revolt was put down and work on the temple recommenced, and a further forty-four years before it was completed; but on 10 September 142 BC, Ptolemy VIII Euergetes II, accompanied by his wife, Cleopatra II, undertook in person its formal dedication.

In 140 BC, Euergetes II ordered a large hypostyle hall of eighteen columns to be added to the southern end of the temple. The hall was completed by 124 BC except for the decoration of its exterior, which was carried out between 116 and 108 BC in the reign of Ptolemy IX Soter II. Soter II ordered the construction of a forecourt and a pylon gateway to the south of the hypostyle hall and of an enclosure wall to surround the whole temple. Work commenced on the new sections of the building in 116 BC and they were dedicated, in spite of the decoration not being finished, in 71 BC by Ptolemy XII Neos Dionysos. Fourteen years later, in 57 BC, the doors of the pylon gateway were hung, marking the completion of Edfu Temple, an achievement that had taken 180 years, three months and fourteen days to accomplish. Work had been carried out according to a coherent design and, by ancient Egyptian standards, over a comparatively short space of time. Thus the Temple can be seen as a complete entity in itself rather than as a sprawling mass such as the edifices at Karnak, which were enlarged and embellished over several hundred years. In spite of the fact that it was built over a period of 180 years, its architecture and decoration have a remarkable unity and harmony; and as it stands today, Edfu Temple is the best preserved in Egypt.

The Different Parts of the Temple

Temples of the Graeco-Roman period, of which Edfu is the archetype, largely conform to what had been the basic plan of a cult temple from the Eighteenth Dynasty (1550-1245 BC) onwards: a massive pylon gateway leading to an open courtyard which in turn led to a large many-columned hall, or hypostyle, erected in front of the sanctuary in which a statue of the god was housed. However, the vocabulary used to describe the different elements of Graeco-Roman temples has become specialized. The innermost part of a temple such as Edfu consisted of a sanctuary encircled by a corridor, or ambulatory, onto which opened a series of rooms and chapels. In front of the sanctuary was a suite of two interconnecting halls flanked by secondary chambers, the most notable of which was the *wabet* (*see* p. 70), the small chapel fronted by a roofless courtyard which was a common feature of temples of the period. In the inscriptions at Edfu the term for the whole sanctuary area was 'Great Seat', but Egyptologists refer to it as the *Naos*, a word that originally meant an open-fronted box shrine containing the divine statue. The columned hall, wider and higher than the rest of the temple, that was built in front of the *Naos*, is known as the *Pronaos*. There is also within a temple enclosure a *mammisi* (*see* below), a structure peculiar to Graeco-Roman temples.

The *Mammisi* at Edfu (8), wherein was commemorated the divine birth of Horus, is situated in the south-west corner of the court in front of the temple. The building is rectangular in shape and consists of an antechamber with a chapel on either side and a staircase on the right leading to the roof; and a main chamber

8   Mammisi, *Edfu Temple*

decorated with scenes connected with the birth of the God. The main chamber is surrounded by a colonnade made up of composite, lotiform and palmiform columns connected with each other by curtain walls, and each having a high abacus decorated on all four sides with the figure of the god, Bes, a suitable motif since Bes was connected with Hathor, to whom the *Mammisi* is dedicated.

From the Pylon Gateway to the north Enclosure Wall, Edfu Temple is just over 140m long and covers an area of over 7000 square metres. The only one of the great Ptolemaic temples to be completed, it is today in an almost perfect state of preservation, with even its roof still intact. Apart from the odd block of stone here and there, only several small roof-chapels, the *cavetto* cornice (*see* Glossary) of the Pylon Gateway's western wing, flagstaffs and the obelisks that were once set before its entrance are missing. The paint which covered the deeply-incised reliefs carved on its walls has worn away; and all the wooden doors that the temple once had, together with metal fixtures such as bolts and clamps, have disappeared, presumably put to good use by the local inhabitants once the temple had been abandoned by its priests.

Like all temples of the period, Edfu was surrounded by auxiliary buildings such as storehouses, kitchens, abbatoirs and administrative offices. One of the most important auxiliary buildings of this or any temple was a structure known as the House of Life, a repository of knowledge about religion, astronomy, medicine and magic. It was also a scriptorium in which novice priests learned the myths and rituals connected with the temple by transcribing the sacred literature into

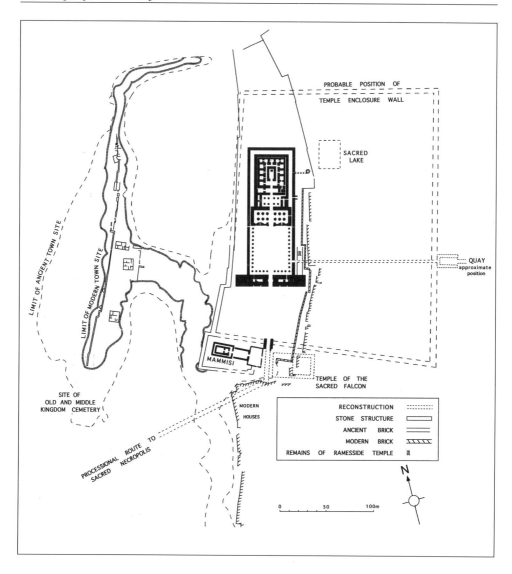

Fig. 2   Plan of Edfu Temple and ancient town

Ptolemaic writing (*see* p. 135). The House of Life at Edfu is thought to have been in or near the main temple enclosure but, sadly, all trace of it has been lost. Today, the temple's auxiliary buildings lie buried under the modern town, as does the sacred lake, the grove in which falcons, considered sacred in the cult of Horus, were reared, and the temple's quay, which was probably on the river bank a short distance to the north of the main building. However, part of the western section of the *temenos* (*see* Glossary), the great mud-brick wall which enclosed the entire temple precinct, still stands.

Two sets of inscriptions in Edfu Temple itself give detailed information about each part of the temple, including its name, purpose and dimensions. These inscriptions, known as the *Building Texts*, are found on the dadoes of the east and west exterior walls of the *Naos*[1] and on the exteriors of the West and East Enclosure Walls.[2] The description of the temple which is given below has been supplemented by information gleaned from the *Building Texts*, quotations from which are sourced in the References at the end of the book. Throughout the description, figures and numerals in brackets refer to the plan of Edfu Temple (*see* p. 68). In the key to the plan, the Arabic numerals in parentheses after the names of parts of the temple refer to the numbered halls and rooms in the plan; the capital letters refer to its doors.

According to the *Building Texts,* the temple was built exactly as it should have been:

> Its length is perfect, its depth is exactly right, its perimeter is the norm, all its measurements have attained perfection. 'Perfect of Proportion' men call it by name. Indeed, its foundations are in the place where they have always been, even as the ancestors ordained for it.[3]

The different parts of the temple conformed to tradition:

> Their chapels are counted, their halls are laid out, their measurements and their columns are as prescribed, (the positions of) their doors are true, their staircases are fixed, the number of their upper chambers is reckoned and their doors are known ….Their walls are correctly placed, beautifully inscribed by the leading craftsmen of the House of Life, all their decorations being carried out according to ancient records. Their ground-plan is exactly as it should be.[4]

The Ptolemaic Temple of Edfu is oriented, unusually, from south to north. Ancient Egyptian temples sited on the west bank of the Nile normally faced east, and those on the east bank faced west, so that their entrances fronted the Nile, facilitating travel on this, the main highway of Egypt. At Edfu, the remains of the pylon gateway of the New Kingdom temple over which the later Ptolemaic structure was erected stand outside the southern end of the East Enclosure Wall of the later building, facing towards the river to the east, thus proving that the earlier temple was oriented east to west. It is probable that the builders of the Ptolemaic temple deliberately chose not to orient it east to west, that is, by the sun, in order to emphasise that Horus of Edfu and the sun-god, Re, were two distinct deities. Today, the temple precinct must be entered from the north, for the modern town has encroached on its southern and eastern sides. Thus the first sight of the temple that a modern visitor has is the outer face of its North Enclosure Wall (**9**).

The North Enclosure Wall, which is nearly 13m high and 50m wide, is decorated on its outer face with huge reliefs depicting the king and queen making

9   *North Enclosure Wall exterior, Edfu Temple*

offerings to the chief deities of the temple, the triad of Horus, Hathor and their son, *Hor-sma-tawy*, perhaps better known by the Greek form of his name, Harsomtus. The figures in the reliefs are arranged as though a vertical line had been drawn on the wall to mark the main axis of the temple, with the figures on one side representing Lower Egypt and those on the other representing Upper Egypt. This concept of duality, with the two halves of the country each represented by its own side of the temple, is largely followed in the arrangement of reliefs throughout the building (*see* p. 43). The invisible axis-line is rather like the spine of an open book, with the page on one side a mirror image of that on the other. The innermost side of each 'page', that is, the side immediately adjacent to the 'spine', was clearly considered the most important, for here the reliefs depict the king holding the figure of the goddess, Maat, in his hand, offering her to Horus and Hathor. Maat stood for Truth, Justice and Social Order, the *raison d'être* of Kingship in ancient Egypt.

Entrance to the temple is made through the Pylon Gateway at its southern end. The modern visitor, therefore, has to walk along the length of either the East or West Enclosure Wall to reach it. These walls are some 130m in length and, like the northern Wall, 13m high. At the base of each is a dado (**10**), which is about 2m high and decorated with the *Building Texts* referred to above. The rest of the Wall is divided horizontally into three registers, and vertically into separate square or rectangular scenes, in which the reliefs show the king making offerings to or performing rites before the gods. Many of the reliefs are damaged, the faces of the

10   *West Enclosure Wall exterior, Edfu Temple: dado of marsh plants with bandeau of* Building Texts *above*

figures chiselled out by Christian or Muslim zealots (*see* p. 108). The most popular deities carved on the walls are Nekhbet, the vulture-goddess of El-Kab, who was the protectress of Upper Egypt; and, of course, Horus himself, chief deity of the temple, sometimes represented as a hawk-headed man, and sometimes as a hawk-headed sphinx protecting the king's *cartouche*. In many of the reliefs in the lowest register, and in some of the *Building Texts*, there are peg-holes. Curtains once hung on the pegs shielding the reliefs under them until the veil was lifted to reveal the deity beneath, presumably to pious visitors who, barred from access to the temple itself, paid for the privilege of beholding the deities under the veils.

The massive Pylon Gateway of Edfu Temple (**11, 12, colour plates 8, 16**) is some 40m in height, a measurement almost matched by the base width of its wings. They flank a 15m high central doorway (A), called the 'Great Inscribed Portal' in the *Building Texts*,[5] surmounted by a balcony, the most important function of which was to provide the point of display for the newly-chosen falcon at the Installation of the Sacred Falcon (*see* p. 100). On either side of the doorway stand two mismatched statues of Horus (**colour plate 18**); and carved into the facade of each wing of the Pylon Gateway are two vertical grooves that once held 'flagstaffs of cedar wood ... worked in bronze from the desert'[6] with 'two great obelisks firm before them'.[7]

11   *Pylon Gateway, Edfu Temple: side view of the west wing with houses of the modern town in the background*

12   *Pylon Gateway, Edfu Temple, showing Ptolemy XII smiting his enemies*

The facade of the Pylon Gateway is decorated with reliefs, with over half of the surface of each wing devoted to the depiction of the traditional scene of the king smiting his enemies. In this instance, a gigantic figure of Ptolemy XII Neos Dionysos, grasping a mace in one, upraised, hand, is shown in the act of slaying his enemies, whom he holds pinioned together by grasping their topknots in his other hand (**12**). Since Neos Dionysos is not known to have waged any wars, these reliefs are purely conventional. Above them are two registers of offering scenes, pierced in several places, to the detriment of the reliefs, by square holes that once held the clamps that supported the flagstaffs (*see* above). The flagstaffs, which were topped by coloured pennons, and painted, would have been well over 45m high, and were only lowered when the God, or his statue at least, was absent from the temple visiting other sanctuaries. The whole ensemble of flagstaffs and the brightly painted reliefs on the Pylon Gateway must have presented an impression of vivid colour.

Inscriptions on the Pylon Gateway were said to contain 'all the rituals for repelling foreigners'[8] but they were unable to protect its great double door, set in place on 5 December 57 BC, from the depredations of later generations of Egyptians. It was too valuable for them to resist removing it, for it was made of cedarwood from the Lebanon and its bronze bolts were made with Asiatic copper. Each leaf of this impressive door was 14m high, 3m wide, and 30cm thick. Every day, at dawn, the door was opened; and every night, at sunset, it was closed: but it was only used for entering the temple on great festival occasions. Otherwise, entrance to the temple Forecourt (1) was made through one of the four doors that were let into the walls of the Enclosure Wall surrounding it, two on the east side, two on the west (**13, 14, 16**). They were 'for coming in and going out, and for enlarging the congregation' and the door (B) 'opposite the Portal of the Golden One, Mistress of Denderah (Hathor)' was 'beautifully decorated'.[9] The Portal of the Golden One (**15**) was only used on the occasion of the sacred marriage between Hathor and Horus of Behdet, for which the statue of the goddess was brought to Edfu from her temple at Denderah. The Portal was 'her beautiful entrance for coming into her house to unite with her image in the Great Seat (*see* p. 106) and for proceeding to her barque to set off in due course for Behdet (i.e. the temple necropolis)'[10] during the Feast of the Joyous Union (*see* Chapter 9).

The paved Forecourt, which is some 50m long by 43m wide, and was called, among other things, the 'Court of Offerings'[11] and the 'Court of the Pylon Gateway,[12] has a covered colonnade on its south, east and west sides. The south colonnade (**colour plate 6**) runs along the rear of the Pylon Gateway, which has a door in each of its wings from which a staircase with 242 steps leads up through the interior to the roof, passing small storage chambers on the way. At the top, the walls are covered with the *graffiti* scrawled by members of Napoleon's 1798 Expedition to Egypt. There are thirty-two columns in the Forecourt's colonnades, twelve on each of its long sides and the rest on the shorter south side, their shafts decorated with sunken reliefs of kings making offerings to the local gods. The decorators chose that the kings should remain nameless for they left the *cartouches*

13   Forecourt, Edfu Temple: door in the north-west wall

14   *Forecourt, Edfu Temple: door in the east wall*

15   Portal of the Golden One, Edfu Temple

16   Forecourt, Edfu Temple: door in the west wall

17   *Forecourt, Edfu Temple: rear of Pylon Gateway, with reliefs of the Ancestral Deities of the temple*

blank (**colour plate 7**). The column capitals are carved in the elaborate floral and palm-leaf designs typical of Ptolemaic temples. Such composite capitals are distinguishing features of Graeco-Roman temples, innovations that identify temples of the period at a glance. In Edfu's Forecourt, and in halls throughout the temple, there is a great variety of decoration in the capitals of the columns, which are arranged symetrically, capitals matching, on either side of the axis, with almost every capital on one side of the Forecourt's axis different from the next.

The walls of the Forecourt are carved with inscriptions and reliefs, many of which depict the sorts of scenes that are endlessly repeated throughout the temple, showing the king making offerings to the gods or slaying enemies. But in several instances they record important temple events and ceremonies. Scenes on the two upper registers of the south wall, the rear wall of the Pylon Gateway (**17**), are concerned with making offerings to the Ancestors, always an important part of temple ceremonial (*see* Chapter 11). In this instance, they are the *Shebtiw*, the ancestral deities of the temple who were thought to be buried in its necropolis. But it is the reliefs on the wall's dado (**18**) that record one of the most important events in the temple's calendar, that of the Feast of the Joyous Union (*see* Chapter 9), for which the statue of Hathor of Denderah was taken to Edfu for her marriage to Horus.

18   *Forecourt, Edfu Temple: text of the Feast of the Joyous Union*

The episodes of the goddess's journey are arranged to the left and right of the doorway as one enters the Forecourt, those on the left presided over by the King of Lower Egypt, wearing the Red Crown, those on the right by the King of Upper Egypt, wearing the White Crown, according to 'rule' (*see* p. 43). The journey by Nile from Denderah to Edfu, and the first day of the Feast, are depicted in reliefs on the right, or eastern, half of the wall. The scenes develop from its eastern end, and the first depicts a flotilla of five ships, sails set for the journey upstream against the current and with the prevailing wind, followed by a scene showing Horus' boat towing Hathor's along the canal leading to the temple. The next scene shows Horus' statue being taken from the Sanctuary, the next shows the statue in its portable shrine being carried to meet Hathor. In the final scene both deities are shown resting in the Sanctuary (**19**). Immediately to the left of the doorway, the reliefs depict the end of the Feast, at which point the portable shrines of Hathor and Horus were placed on board their ships ready for the journey to the borders of the Edfu district where Horus turned back for home while Hathor sailed on to Denderah (**20**). Her return voyage was downstream, with the current, and so the reliefs show the ships with their sails furled. The final scene (**21**), which is carved west of the doorway into the Pylon Gateway, shows men dancing to the accompaniment of women shaking rattles.

19   *Forecourt, Edfu Temple: Hathor's portable shrine resting in the Sanctuary during the Feast of the Joyous Union*

20   Forecourt, Edfu Temple: Hathor's journey home to Denderah

The dadoes[13] of the east and west walls of the Forecourt are decorated with representations of all forty-two administrative districts of Egypt. Each of the districts is represented by four figures, two female and two male. The first female carries in her hand the emblem of her district. Behind her is a man personifying a canal; behind him a female personifying agricultural land; and behind her a man personifying marshland, all vital features of Egypt's landscape. Each group of four is linked to an appropriate scene carved on the top, that is, the third register on the east[14] and west walls.[15] Led by the king, they all face towards the northern end of the Forecourt where, in the angle of the wall, Horus, Hathor and their son, *Hor-sma-tawy*, are depicted waiting to greet them.

The district representatives on each wall form what might be termed a geographical procession. Beginning at the southern end of the west wall, the first scene is concerned with the Soped or twentieth district of Lower Egypt, that at the southern end of the east wall with the Knife or twenty-second district of Upper Egypt. Each district of Lower and Upper Egypt is then represented in a scene on the west or east wall as appropriate, culminating with the last scene at the northern end of each wall, that on the west representing Memphis, the first district of Lower Egypt, and that on the east Elephantine, the first district of Upper Egypt. Although the inscriptions do not explicitly state the fact, it seems reasonable to suppose that the list of the districts in the geographical procession carved on the

1   *Head of Horus*

2   *Temple of Horus and Sobek at Kom Ombo*

3 *(opposite)*   *Sobek: relief in First Hypostyle Hall at Kom Ombo*

4   Pronaos, *Edfu Temple:* cavetto *cornice and* torus *roll*

5 *(opposite)*   Pronaos, *Edfu Temple: interior*

6   *Forecourt, Edfu Temple: south colonnade*

7 *(opposite)*   *Forecourt, Edfu Temple: column with empty* cartouche

8   *Pylon Gateway, Edfu Temple*

9 (opposite)   Pronaos, *Edfu Temple: statue of Horus with screen wall in background*

10   Western stairway, Denderah Temple: procession of priests

11 (opposite)   King Ay acting as sem-*priest, tomb of Tutankhamun*

12   North Enclosure Wall, Edfu temple: procession of Sacred Falcon

13   Denderah Temple: Hathor suckling her son Harsomtus

14   *West Enclosure Wall, Edfu Temple:* The Triumph of Horus, *Act II, Scene i*

15   Pronaos, *Esna Temple: Baptism of Pharaoh*

16   Edfu Temple in AD 1834: exterior view. Lithograph by David Roberts

*17 (opposite)   The Temple of Khnum at Esna: interior in AD 1843. Painting by the
German Egyptologist, Richard Lepsius (1810-1884)*

18   *Horus Falcon: one of the mismatched pair of colossal granite statues set before the Pylon of Edfu Temple*

21   Forecourt, Edfu Temple: final scene of the Feast of the Joyous Union

walls of the Forecourt was read out in a roll call that was held as the culminating ritual of the New Year Festival (*see* Chapter 7) or of any celebration in which a rededication of the districts, and therefore of Egypt, was called for. Thus, after the rituals had been celebrated in the temple, the ceremonial procession would make its way into the Forecourt where the district representatives, either in person or symbolized by the reliefs on the walls, would be drawn up facing them.

The east and west exterior walls of the Forecourt are prolonged round the *Pronaos* and *Naos* on the north side to form the Enclosure Wall, with the space between it and the exterior of the north, west and east sides of the *Naos* forming a corridor known as the Pure Ambulatory. From beneath the pavement on the eastern side of the corridor a flight of steps leads under the Enclosure Wall to a well, which supplied the temple with its daily requirements of water. The inner surface of the Enclosure Wall is covered in reliefs and inscriptions, the most famous of which is on its west surface, and is the 'script' of *The Triumph of Horus over His Enemies* (*see* p. 113), the ritual play that was acted annually at Edfu. In the eastern corner of the north wall is the inscription naming Imhotep as architect of the temple (*see* p. 46). The exteriors of the north, east and west walls of the *Naos* are decorated with hieroglyphic texts and elaborate reliefs carved *en creux* . There are three lion-headed gargoyles (*see* p. 40) on each of the east and west walls, and two on the north wall (**23**). Along the bottom of all three walls runs a dado of Nile

22   *Forecourt, Edfu Temple: view towards the* Pronaos

23   Naos, *Edfu Temple: exterior, showing gargoyles*

gods and offering bearers surmounted by two lines of dedicatory inscriptions, the *Building Texts* (*see* p. 51); and the tops of the walls are decorated with friezes containing *cartouches* and winged and crowned cobras.

The outer Hypostyle Hall, or *Pronaos* (2), which is higher and wider than the *Naos* beyond, lies to the north of the Forecourt (**22**). Its ceiling is decorated with astronomical motives, and its walls are 'beautifully inscribed'[16] although the reliefs are not so fine as those in the inner hypostyle or Great Hall (5). Apart from the great central doorways in the south and north walls, the *Pronaos* has 'a small door in it, to the east, and 18 beautiful columns (**colour plate 5**) uplifting the roof.'[17] Twelve of these columns are free-standing in the Hall, with the rest incorporated into the south wall as engaged columns, three on either side of the broken-lintel doorway. The south wall of the *Pronaos* is a fine example of a Ptolemaic screen wall (**colour plate 9**). This type of wall had been in use since the Eighteenth Dynasty, notably in the small temple at Medinet Habu built in the reigns of Hatshepsut (1479-1457 BC) and Thutmose III (1479-1425 BC), and in the Temple of Ptah at Karnak. They may have been introduced into Egypt by Thutmose III, possibly inspired by the temples he saw in his military campaigns in Syria-Palestine, where screen walls were necessary to protect the interior of a temple from climatic conditions that were more inclement than those in Egypt. By the Late Period, screen walls were a popular architectural conceit. The screen wall of the *Pronaos* in a Ptolemaic temple did, however, shield the interior of the *Pronaos* from the unauthorized gaze of participants in certain temple ceremonies during which they were allowed into the Forecourt but no further.

At Edfu, the screen wall rises to about half the height of the columns forming the south wall of the *Pronaos*. Two small chapels, which are entered from inside the *Pronaos*, are built into the thickness of the wall, one to the left (west) of the entrance, the other to the right (east). The chapel to the left is the House of the Morning (3), in which the King or his deputy was purified before performing any ritual.[18] Reliefs on its walls show the purification of the King being performed, as was usual, by a *sem*-priest, (*see* p. 76) distinguished by the leopard-skin worn over one shoulder. There is also a scene of the King being purified by Horus and Thoth, the so-called 'Baptism of Pharaoh' (*see* p. 124). The chapel to the right is the House of Books (4), or temple library, where the sacred books of the temple were deposited in the form of rolls of papyrus or leather which were kept in containers and placed in niches in the walls of the room. They have, of course, long-since disappeared, and in their stead we have a list of their titles, arranged in columns engraved on the side walls of the chapel as follows:

> The books and the great parchments of pure leather for
> bringing about the overthrowing of the Evil One, the
> repelling of the Crocodile (Seth), the blessing of the hour,
> the preservation of a boat, the procession of the great boat.
> The book for setting the King off on procession.
> The book for performing the ritual for the protection of the
> city, of the houses, of the White Crown, of the year.

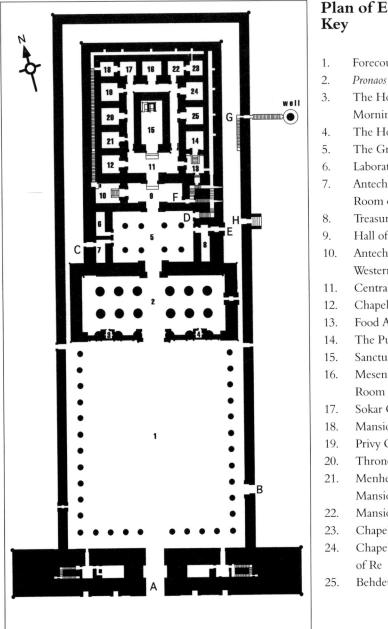

Plan of Edfu Temple: Key

1.   Forecourt
2.   *Pronaos*
3.   The House of the Morning
4.   The House of Books
5.   The Great Hall
6.   Laboratory
7.   Antechamber-The Room of the Nile
8.   Treasury
9.   Hall of Offerings
10.   Antechamber to Western Stairway
11.   Central Hall
12.   Chapel of Min
13.   Food Altar
14.   The Pure Place
15.   Sanctuary
16.   Mesen (Harpoon) Room
17.   Sokar Chamber
18.   Mansion of the Prince
19.   Privy Chamber
20.   Throne of the Gods
21.   Menhet (Raiment) Mansion
22.   Mansion of the Leg
23.   Chapel of Hathor
24.   Chapel of the Throne of Re
25.   Behdet (Throne) Room

Fig. 3   *The Temple of Edfu (after Chassinat)*

The book for appeasing the goddess Sekhmet.
The book for hunting the lion, repelling crocodiles,
driving away reptiles; knowing the secrets of the
Laboratory; knowing all the details about the divine
offerings, all the lists of the secret forms of the god and
all the aspects of the associated deities, copied for the
temple day after day, one after the other, for the souls of
the deities which live in this place and never leave this temple.
The book of the temple inventory.
The book of capturing enemies.
The book of marshal combat.
The book of temple regulations.
The roll book of temple guards.
Instructions for the decoration of a wall; the protection of
the body.
The book of magical protection of the King in his palace.
Formulae for warding off the Evil Eye.
Information about the regular appearance of two stars
(that is, the sun and the moon) and the periodical return
of the other stars.
Enumeration of all the sacred places and knowledge
about what is in them.
All the rituals concerning the God leaving his temple on
feast days.[19]

A reader-priest was on duty in the library 'for the twelve hours of the day'.[20]

Beyond the *Pronaos*, to its north, are the halls and chapels which formed the original nucleus of the temple, the *Naos*. First, the Great Court (5) or inner hypostyle hall, which has twelve columns, all of which are free-standing. They are more slender than those in the *Pronaos*, with the lower part of the shaft being narrower than the rest of the column. The Great Court had several names: it was called the 'Place of Delectation', the 'Place of Heart's Desire', and the 'Pleasure House of Re and Horus.'[21] The 'House of Enjoyment' and the 'House of Satisfaction' were two more of its names; and, as the names indicate, it was said to be the 'place within which the God enjoys himself'.[22] In its north-west corner is a chapel (6) 'complete with the work of the Master of the Laboratory'.[23] The work consisted of preparing incense and unguents for use in the temple, and the walls of the chapel, or Laboratory, are inscribed with recipes for these preparations.

To the south of the Laboratory, in the south-west corner of the Great Court, is an Antechamber (7). This room has two doors, one leading to the Great Court, the other (C) leading to the Pure Ambulatory, the corridor that runs round the exterior of the west, north and east sides of the *Naos*. The Antechamber was known as the Room of the Nile, and through Door C water for libations was brought into the temple every day. In the north-east corner of the Great Court lies the entrance (D) to a winding stairway that leads to the roof of the *Naos*. To the south of this stairway is a passage (E) through which the Daily Offerings were brought into the temple; and to the south of the passage, opening into it, lies the Treasury (8). This was the 'beautiful place for gold, silver, precious stones and the amulets used for protection.'[24]

The Great Court leads to the Hall of Offerings (9) which is 'inscribed in the interior with the ritual of the divine service (*see* Chapter 6) and all the rites appropriate to it'.[25] On the Hall's eastern side is a winding stairway (F), and on the western side a straight stairway, approached through an antechamber (10). The God 'went forth by the eastern stairway wearing his great crown, with his Ennead (company of gods) behind him, in order to look at the sun's disk and to unite with his Ba ('soul') on New Year's Day'.[26] When the New Year's Day ceremonies on the roof (*see* p. 95) were ended, the God came down and 'entered his sanctuary by the right-hand stairway to the west'.[27] The walls on either side of each stairway are decorated with reliefs depicting priests carrying the sacred standards and portable shrines; the steps, shallow enough to make the carrying easier, are worn, an evocative reminder of the passage of countless pairs of feet.

To the north of the Hall of Offerings is the Central Hall (11), the 'Place Where the Gods Repose'.[28] It was in this Hall that the statues of the co-templar gods and goddesses were housed, each in its own portable shrine. On the west of the Central hall is the Chapel of Min (12), the ithyphallic god of fertility, in which he appears in the guise of Min-Amun, to represent fertility, and Min-Horus, to express royalty. The purpose of this chapel was probably to reinforce the concept of royalty, one of the *raisons d'être* of the temple. On the east of the Central Hall lies a square room, open to the sky, with a door on its north side leading up a flight of six steps to another square room. The facade of the upper room is largely composed of a screen wall and a column with elaborate floral capitals on either side of a broken-lintel doorway. The screen walls and the fact that the top of the door is some way from the top of the columns allows light to enter the upper chamber and illuminate its ceiling, which shows the sky-goddess, Nut, swallowing the sun at dusk and giving birth to it at dawn. The lower room was called the Food Altar (13), the upper the Pure Place or *wabet* (14), and it was in these chambers that the preliminary rites of the Festival of Raiment and the New Year Festival were performed. Reliefs in the Pure Place show Ptolemy VIII Euergetes II and his Queen making offerings to his ancestor, Ptolemy III Euergetes I, and his Queen, (*see* p. 129) while other reliefs show the reigning King and Queen being worshipped by the blue-painted images of two dead kings.

The north wall of the Central Hall is actually the facade of the Sanctuary (15), known as the 'Great Seat'(**24**). Access to the successive halls of the temple was progessively denied, and only the King, or his deputy, the High Priest, was allowed to enter the inner sanctum. The Sanctuary, which is a rectangular room complete with its own roof set within the main body of the *Naos*, has a corridor running round its east, north and west sides which is lit by small apertures in the ceiling. Its facade is inscribed with the morning litany (*see* p. 82) which was sung

24   *Sanctuary, Edfu Temple: shrine with boat pedestal in front*

during the Daily Ritual. Today, the stone pedestal on which the portable shrine of Horus rested, joined by that of Hathor when the goddess was a guest at Edfu, if the reliefs on the side walls of the chamber are to be taken literally, still sits in the middle of the room. The Sanctuary also held the 'great shrine of black stone'[29] presented to the pre-Ptolemaic temple by Nectanebo II. During Mariette's excavations (*see* page 131), the shrine was found standing off-centre within the Sanctuary, and was repositioned in what was presumed to be its original position in the centre of the room, behind the pedestal for the portable shrine. It was originally closed by means of bronze doors, now lost, and held the cult statue of Horus, which was probably about 60cm high and made of wood overlaid with gold and set with semi-precious stones. Today, the vista from the shrine opens out along the length of the temple's axis to the Forecourt; but such a vista would have been impossible when the wooden doors of the temple were still in place.

The corridor which runs round the exterior of the Sanctuary gives access to the small chapels, known as the 'Mysterious Portals',[30] which lie on its east, north and west sides. The most important of these chapels (16) lies directly on the axis of the temple, immediately behind the Sanctuary. It was called the 'Mesen (Harpoon) Room'[31] or the 'Mansion of Valour'.[32] A statue of Horus as Re-Horakhty stood within the Mesen Room, together with a statue of Hathor, each placed within 'a mysterious shrine of black stone'.[33] Beside them stood the 'Falcon of Gold in his shrine';[34] and two sacred lances.[35] Today, a model of the barque of Horus stands in the Mesen Room: it was built for a re-enactment of the divine ritual staged by the English Egyptologist, Arthur Weigall (1880-1934), who was Chief Inspector of Antiquities for Upper Egypt between 1905 and 1914.

Three chapels situated in the north-west corner of the corridor were devoted to the cult of Osiris, the most popular of Egyptian gods, who was originally a deity of agriculture and fertility but who, thanks to his murder at the hands of his brother, Seth, followed by his resurrection, became chief deity of the Underworld. On the west of the Mesen Room lies the Sokar Chamber (17). Sokar was originally an agricultural deity whose main centre of worship was in the area around Memphis. From an early date he was regarded as the guardian of the Memphite necropolis, and was also linked with Ptah, the patron deity of Memphis. Thanks to similarities in the natures of Sokar and Osiris, both being funerary deities with agricultural associations, all three gods eventually coalesced into a deity worshipped as Ptah-Sokar-Osiris; and by the Ptolemaic period, Sokar had become little more than a variant of Osiris.

Opening out of the Sokar Chamber is an annexe (18) known as the 'Mansion of the Prince'.[36] The two rooms were together called the 'Portals of the Pillar-god (Osiris)'.[37] In the first, which was supposed to represent the tomb of the god in Memphis, Osiris' wife Isis is shown reassembling the pieces of her dead husband's body after it had been dismembered by Seth. In the second, which represents the god's sanctuary at Heliopolis, the ancient Osiris mysteries[38] are recorded in the reliefs, the most important of which shows Osiris seated on the throne celebrating his *Heb-Sed* or Jubilee Festival. To the south of the annexe is the so-called Privy Chamber (19) which was devoted to Osiris in association with Isis and their sister, Nephthys. The Sokar Chamber, its annexe and the Privy Chamber were together known as the 'Palaces of the Pillar-god in Behdet'[39] and have their counterparts at Denderah and Philae, although in these temples the suite of Osiris chambers is on the roof. To the south of the Privy Chamber is the Throne of the Gods (20), in which the divine ennead of Edfu was worshipped; and the Menhet Mansion (21) or Raiment Room, which contained the cadaster of the administrative districts and the coloured cloths required during the daily service.

On the eastern side of the corridor that runs round the Sanctuary, next to the Mesen Chamber, lies the Mansion of the Leg (22), which has a door in its east wall leading to the Chapel of Hathor (23), called in the inscriptions 'a magazine'[40]. The Mansion of the Leg was devoted to Khonsu of Behdet, otherwise known as Khonsu, the moon-god son of Amun and Mut. The Leg was the left leg of Osiris, in other places said to be the mythological source of the Nile at Philae, but here worshipped in the form of a reliquary shaped like an obelisk. Both rooms are concerned with the mythology of the source of the Nile, and with the annual rising of the Dog Star, Sothis. The ancient Egyptians realized at an early date that the Nile began to rise on or about the same date each year, that is, near 19th July in the Julian calendar; and that Sothis, having been invisible for a long time, was again observed on the horizon just before sunrise. Thus, the rising of Sothis, termed the heliacal rising of Sirius by modern astronomers, marked the beginning of the Egyptian year, New Year's Day.

To the south of the Chapel of Hathor lies the Throne of Re (24), in which the soul of Re was supposed to sleep at night and from which the god was said to rise each morning; and the Throne Room (25), or Behdet Room, which is decorated with images of the goddess Mehyt. She was the daughter of Re, represented in the form of a fierce lioness, who, with the aid of other deities, protected the roads along which the deceased must journey to reach the Underworld. The purpose of the images of Mehyt in the Throne Room was to protect Behdet, the temple of Horus, by propitiatory offerings of incense. On the left side of her sacred barque a hymn describes her as angry and aggressive; but the hymn on the right extols her as a peacable and beneficent goddess.

According to the *Building Texts*, the temple was furbished by Horus of Behdet himself:

> He has enriched its treasuries with numerous requirements of gold and silver. He has stocked its granaries with barley and emmer in excess of the daily rations, and has equipped its storehouses with servants ceaselessly performing their tasks. He has filled its byres to overflowing with long- and short-horned cattle, to supply their daily portions, and provided its bird-pools with plump fowl so as to be able to present their choice parts to the temple.[41]

5 Priesthood and the Daily Ritual

The Priesthood

In over three millennia of changing political regimes, economic circumstances and social conditions, one aspect of ancient Egyptian life remained constant, and that was the Egyptians' attachment to their religious beliefs and conventions. Priests, therefore, were important members of society. They were not, however, spiritual leaders in the way that Christian and Muslim clergy are, they were not preachers, they had no congregations. Since there were no sacred books such as the Bible or the Koran in Egypt, there was no need for priests to be interpreters of such books. Unlike rabbis, they were not expected to be authorities on religious law and doctrine. An Egyptian priest observed religious law as practised in his own temple, and it was the doctrine of his own temple that he was most familiar with. Priests were not even required to exert moral authority or to have a divine calling to the priesthood, for their role was to carry out the temple rituals necessary for the maintenance of cosmic order and the well-being of Egypt, not as agents in their own right but in the name of the King, who was considered to be the High Priest of every temple.

The King was believed to be both god and man. He could, as a human being, worship himself as a divinity; and to his subjects he was the incarnation of every god revered throughout Egypt, a deity in living form whom they could see, speak to and adore. The King was accepted by other gods as one of them; and as High Priest he addressed them not as a supplicant but as an equal. In the rites depicted on the walls of a temple, the King makes offerings to the gods not in order to propitiate them but almost on a business footing, in the spirit of *quid pro quo*. If a king offers a god wine, he expects the god to reply in kind and offer him the vines upon which the grapes that make the wine grow; if he offers a goddess perfume, he expects her to provide him with love and happiness in return; and if he offers a god 'the field' (*see* p. 127), he expects the god to confirm his ownership of Egypt.

Priests, like everybody who was associated in any way with the divine cult, had to be pure, if not entirely in mind certainly in body. The term used to describe the lowest rank of priest, *w'b*, which means 'purified', reflects this. Before entering a cult temple, a priest had to clean his mouth with natron (sodium carbonate or bicarbonate) diluted with water, and wash himself, either in the sacred lake (**25**), or, where there was no lake, in a special stone tank set aside for the purpose. The Greek historian, Herodotus, who visited Egypt in the fifth century BC, noted that

25   Sacred Lake, Denderah Temple

when on duty priests were accustomed to 'bathe in cold water twice a day and twice every night'.[1] The hands with which they held cult vessels and touched divine statues received special attention, finger nails being cut short and dirt removed from them; and the feet on which they walked on sacred ground were likewise cleaned, and toenails trimmed. Rigorous depilation was a requirement, with every hair of the body removed. Herodotus stated that priests shaved their bodies all over every other day 'to guard against lice or anything equally unpleasant'.[2] From the Eighteenth Dynasty priests had been required to shave their heads; and this became such a strict obligation in the Graeco-Roman period that any priest who failed to observe it was fined 1000 drachma, probably the equivalent of an agricultural worker's wages for about 50 days.

Priests were allowed to dress only in linen and never in leather or wool from living animals which, it was believed, would contaminate the holy places. Through the ages, the basic priestly costume of a kilt stretching from mid-calf to above the waist, held up by two broad shoulder-straps, did not vary and was worn by all ranks (**colour plate 10**). Long before Graeco-Roman times it had become archaic. A detail of dress, such as the sash a reader-priest wore across his chest, sometimes marked the priest's function; otherwise it was only specialized priests who wore a different costume. The *sem*-priest, whose chief duty was to officiate at funerary ceremonies, was distinguished by the animal-skin, which could be that of a cheetah or the more highly-valued leopard, draped across his shoulders (**colour plate 11**); the High Priest of Memphis wore a special collar and a plait of hair on one side of his head, and the High Priest of Heliopolis wore a panther-skin patterned with stars. From as early as the Ninth Dynasty, priests wore white sandals, outside the sacred precincts at least; and the wearing of sandals, in a country where it was usual to walk barefoot, was interpreted by Greek and Roman writers as a priestly privilege.

The same writers misinterpreted the dietary restrictions of the priesthood, claiming that many foods were forbidden to its members. Chaeremon stated that Egyptian priests did not eat cow meat or pigeons, Flavius Josephus and Plutarch that they did not eat pork, Aristagoras that they did not eat sheep; and Horapollo that they did not eat pelicans, although these were not a delicacy that many Egyptians desired to consume. Plutarch claimed that they did not eat vegetables or garlic, Herodotus that they did not eat beans. It seems more likely, however, that all these vegetables and animals were proscribed only in certain places, each for their own mythological reasons. Every district of Egypt worshipped its own deity, often in the form of a sacred animal. For example, a jackal was worshipped in the Seventeenth District of Upper Egypt, known to the Greeks as Cynopolis or City of the Dogs. A short distance to the north of Cynopolis lay a town in which Seth was worshipped in the form of a *Mormyrus*- or *Oxyrhynchus*-fish, which according to legend swallowed the penis of Osiris after Seth had thrown it into the Nile. Naturally, no inhabitant of the city of Oxyrhynchus, let alone a priest, would dream of eating an *Oxyrhynchus*-fish, although in places where the fish was not held to be sacred it may have formed part of the normal diet. Lack of respect for local taboos was sometimes a cause of friction, as Plutarch relates: 'In our time, the people of Oxyrhynchus, because the people of Cynopolis had eaten an *Oxyrhynchus*-fish, seized some dogs and killed and ate them. From this came a war.'[3]

Priests seem not to have had any special training; nor were they required to demonstrate any particular talent for priesthood except the willingness to undertake its disciplines. Priests were not expected to be unmarried, but they were obliged to refrain from sexual intercourse during each period of service. The same obligations were required of women as well as men, for there were priestesses, especially in temples devoted to goddesses such as Hathor. In the Graeco-Roman period, male candidates for the priesthood were circumcised, for, according to Herodotus, they 'preferred to be clean rather than comely';[4] and under the Emperor Hadrian, who decreed that only priests could be circumcised, circumcision became a priest's distinguishing mark. It is not clear, however, to what extent circumcision was practised in the Pharaonic period.

Up to the Middle Kingdom, many priests, especially those in the lowest category, were the sons of non-priestly parents. But by the Twentieth Dynasty, and in some cases as early as Dynasty XII, priestly status seems to have become hereditary, with purely priestly families coming into being. Later on, perhaps as early as the Twenty-sixth Dynasty, and certainly by the Ptolemaic period, admittance to the priesthood was restricted to persons of priestly descent. The

High Priest of a temple was appointed by the King; other categories of priest were appointed in a variety of ways: by the King or his representative, such as the local governor or the High Priest; or by deed of transfer from one priest to another. A priestly office could be inherited; and it could be purchased. By Roman times, if not earlier, there were very strict tests for admittance to the priesthood: a would-be entrant had to prove that both his father and grandfather were or had been priests, and that he was free from bodily defects. In Roman times, a man who was of priestly descent, unblemished in body and circumcised, had to pay a fee to the State for the privilge of being admitted to the priesthood. Many felt that it was worth it. Although the priestly life implied duties and demanded a certain discipline, especially with regard to ritual purity, it also conferred privileges, not least the certainty of food and shelter.

Priests were not necessarily exempt from State forced labour such as work on digging canals, building dykes or even hewing stone in quarries; but the priests of certain temples were granted immunity from all such labour by special royal decree. In the Old Kingdom, temples were subjected to imposts such as the provisioning of officials engaged in royal commissions, thus losing some of their income. By the New Kingdom, some temples had won exemption from such costly exercises. Priests had the right of asylum within their temples, although this was curtailed in the Roman period in return for the immunity from poll tax that had first been granted in the Ptolemaic period. Priests received a share of the offerings that came into the temple every day, and were paid a regular income from its estates, with the priests of the largest, richest, temples benefitting most. The offerings were divided on a daily basis, with each priest receiving a greater or lesser share according to his rank: the normal share for a High Priest was one tenth. A priest's daily rations, according to Herodotus, consisted of bread and 'a great quantity of goose-meat and beef, in addition to wine'.[5] The wives and daughters of priests also received a daily bread allowance. A High Priest had special perquisites: in the Temple of Wepwawet at Lycopolis (modern Assiut), for example, the High Priest received a roast of meat from every bull slaughtered and a portion of beer from every jar used on days when there was a procession. Other priests supplemented their income by performing services for the dead.

There were several categories of priest in a cult temple, the lowest being the *w'b*-priest. Every entrant to the priesthood, even the son of a king, had to begin his career as a *w'b*-priest. The next rank was that of 'father-of-the-god' (*it-ntr*). The higher ranking priests were known as 'servants of the god' or *ḥm-ntr*, an apt description since a temple was supposed to be the house of a god, putting its priests on a par with domestic servants. The Greeks called the *ḥm-ntr* priests 'prophets', but these priests are not to be confused in any way with the Prophets of the Old Testament. There were three categories of *ḥm-ntr*, the third *ḥm-ntr* being the lowest in rank, the first *ḥm-ntr* being the High Priest of the temple. The history of Bakenkhons,[6] High Priest of Amun at Thebes in the time of Ramesses II (1279-1213 BC), is a wonderful example of a very successful career in the priesthood! At the age of one, Bakenkhons became a pupil in the Temple of Mut at Thebes. Since the normal age for starting school was six, this either means that he was an orphan or was dedicated as an infant to the priesthood. At the age of ten, Bakenkhons was apprenticed to the training stables of Ramesses' father, Sety I, until, aged fifteen, he entered the service of Amun as a *w'b*-priest. Four years later, Bakenkhons became an *it-ntr*, a rank he occupied for twelve years until, at the age of thirty-two, he became third *ḥm-ntr*. He remained third *ḥm-ntr* for fifteen years, and then, aged forty-seven, became second *ḥm-ntr*. After twelve years as second *ḥm-ntr*, the fifty-nine year old Bakenkhons was elevated to first *ḥm-ntr*. He remained High Priest of Amun for twenty-seven years until his death at the age of eighty-six, having spent seventy-one years as a priest.

The priesthood of a cult temple was divided into four groups, known as *s3w* or 'gangs' in ancient Egyptian but as phylae in Greek, with each phyle serving one lunar month in four. At the end of its month's duty, the outgoing phyle drew up an inventory of temple property and checked it with the incoming phyle. It is difficult to establish how many priests normally made up a phyle, but in the Graeco-Roman Temple of Sobek at Soknopaios in the Faiyum there were thirty-one priests to each phyle, a number that was evidently felt to be insufficient by Ptolemy III, who added a fifth phyle, a system that lasted until the final closure of the pagan temples. Each phyle had a superintendant whom the Greeks called a phylarch. In Pharaonic times, any priest, be he *w'b*, father- or servant-of-the-god, was eligible to be phylarch; but in the Graeco-Roman period a phylarch had to hold the rank of servant-of-the-god.

Certain positions in a cult temple were held by full-time members of staff who did not belong to the rotating phylae but were on duty at all times. The post of Superintendant of the temple, held by the High Priest, was permanent, as was that of chief Reader-priest, whose duty it was to recite from the sacred books when occasion demanded. Both posts were often held by the same man. The priests known as *s3-mry.f* (son-whom-he-loves), who performed the Opening of the Mouth Ceremony (*see* p. 90) and the *iwn-mwt.f* (pillar-of-his-mother), who featured in coronations, jubilees and royal processions, were permanent members of staff, as were the door-keepers, temple-sweepers and other minor officials.

In the earliest periods of Egyptian history, the administration of cult temples seems to have been much more in the hands of the laity than was the case later on, although even at this time the governing body of a temple was a small committee, known as a *ḳnbt*, which was composed entirely of priests. Almost every man, or woman, of any importance held a priestly appointment in addition to his secular office, and took an active part in the ceremonial life of the local cult temple. Part-time priests belonging to a so-called *wnwt* or 'hour-priesthood', which seems to have been a group of unpaid laymen, took part in the processions that were held during the great festivals, and appointed one of their number every month to serve in the temple. By the New Kingdom, however, laypeople were totally excluded from worship in the cult temples. Administration was still the responsibility of a *ḳnbt*, but it was firmly under the control of the High Priest; and in the Graeco-Roman period, temples were ruled by committees until AD 202 when they were placed under the control of the municipal senates.

Although a priest was not given any special training or guidance on what was expected of him before entering the priesthood, inscriptions in Edfu Temple on the jambs of the doors through which priests entered every day instructed them on priestly behaviour. On one doorjamb, priests are enjoined not to present themselves in a state of sin, not to enter the temple in a state of impurity and not to speak lies in the house of the god. The priests are further exhorted: 'Do not hold back supplies, or collect taxes that injure the unimportant in favour of the mighty. Do not add to the weights and measures but make them smaller ... reveal nothing that you see in any secret matter of the sanctuaries.'[7] On another doorjamb, the priests are told that Horus bids them to:

> Enter in peace, leave in peace, go in happiness. For life is in His hand, peace is in His grasp, all good things are with Him. There is food for him who remains at His table, and nourishment for him who partakes of His offerings. No misfortune or evil will befall the one who lives on His beneficence, neither is there damnation for the one who serves Him for His care reaches to heaven and His security to earth and His protection is greater than that of all the gods.[8]

The Daily Ritual in Edfu Temple

The Daily Ritual was celebrated in the Temple of Edfu in three services, performed in the morning, at midday and in the evening, of which the Morning Service was the most and the Midday Service the least important. Judging by the great calendar in the memorial temple of Ramesses III at Medinet Habu, which distinguishes between the normal daily ritual and that of the 'festivals of the sky' and the 'festivals of the times' or calendar feasts, it is very likely that on certain days the morning service in particular was celebrated with more pomp and ceremony than on others. Nothing is known, however, about these occasions at Edfu. Of the rites that were performed during the standard Daily Ritual,[9] nineteen are engraved on parts of the east and west interior walls of the Sanctuary.[10] Lack of space must have dictated that only a selection of the most important rituals be recorded, with others, such as the kindling of the fire necessary for the burning of incense, omitted.

The Morning Service took place at dawn. In preparation for the Service, and indeed for the whole day, all the doors of the temple were opened 'at daybreak when the sun's rays illumine the earth'[11], with the doors of the Pylon Gateway being 'opened in the morning at sunrise and only closed at evening-time'.[12] Long before dawn, however, the priests would have been up and about making preparations. Two brought water from the well (G) located in the eastern part of the Pure Ambulatory (**26**); then with one priest carrying the water in a jar and the other walking in front wafting incense over it,[13] they walked around the northern end of the Ambulatory to its western side where they entered the temple by the

26   *Eastern Ambulatory, Edfu Temple: floor-level entrance to sacred well*

door (C) that leads into the Chamber of the Nile (7). At the door and in the Chamber of the Nile the water was consecrated before being carried into the Inner Hypostyle Hall (5). The two priests then used the water to replenish every libation vessel.

Meantime, in the kitchens that lay to the east of the temple, the god's 'breakfast' was being prepared. This consisted of a roasted ox and other meats, and vegetables. When they were ready they were carried through the door (H) in the Enclosure Wall and into the Inner Hypostyle (5) through the door (E) in its eastern wall. There they were purified with incense and then taken into the Hall of Offerings (9). Some were carried to the Hall of the Ennead (11) for 'consumption' by the co-templar deities whose shrines were housed there. Every priest taking part in the preparation and distribution of the offerings for the Morning Service had first purified himself at the Sacred Lake.

Just before daybreak, with everything in readiness for the Morning Service to commence, the chief officiant, in theory the King himself but in practice presumably the senior priest on duty, passed through the main door of the Pronaos. As he did so he recited the text inscribed on the thickness of each door-jamb, which is an abbreviated version of the Declaration of Innocence,[14] normally a long recitation of sins not committed that a dead person spoke at his judgement before the gods of the Afterlife to ensure his eternal life. The officiant then turned to the left and made his way to the House of the Morning (*see* p. 67), where he was ceremonially purified and dressed in his vestments. He also ate a light meal. Then, to the accompaniment of priests chanting hymns, he made his way to the inner sanctum, the Sanctuary (15), the doors of which were closed and sealed, the shrine containing the statue of Horus safely inside.

As the doors of the Sanctuary swung open, the Morning Hymn was sung. The text[15] of this great hymn is engraved in twelve sections upon the facade of the Sanctuary.[16] The four less important sections are squeezed onto the narrow wall-surface behind the carved *torus*-roll (*see* Glossary) at each corner of the facade and into narrow strips at the inner edges of the reliefs on either side of the door. A further two texts are carved above these reliefs. The six remaining texts, which are the most important, are carved in the top half of the facade to the left and right of the *torus*-roll, three to each side. They actually make up one consecutive litany. The sections of hymn in the top two reliefs to the right of the *torus*-roll are addressed to Horus of Behdet; the section under them to the other deities worshipped in his temple. The sections of hymn to the left of the *torus*-roll are addressed to various parts of Horus' body, to the emblems and ornaments worn or carried by him, to the halls, chapels, pillars and gates of his temple, to the reliefs carved upon its walls, and to the boat-shrine in which the god rested. The hymn bids them all to 'awake in peace'.

The priests who chanted the Morning Hymn were probably joined by priestesses who accompanied the singing by clacking large bead necklaces, called *menit*, and shaking sistra, loops of metal with rods crossing from one side of the loop to the other, each threaded with metal beads that were left loose in their sockets so that they rattled when shaken. The Morning Hymn as engraved on the facade of the Sanctuary is very long, and it was surely not sung in its entirety every day. Once it, or an abbreviated version, had been sung, the officiant entered the Sanctuary in which the statue of Horus, which had been shut up in its shrine since the Evening Service of the previous day, awaited him. Horus and his co-templar divinities, his regalia, the temple itself and the reliefs on its walls were all thought of as separate animate beings who slept during the hours of darkness. Thus when the doors of the Sanctuary were shut for the night, the whole temple slept until dawn. The purpose of the Morning Service was to awaken it.

The officiant began the Service by breaking the clay seals on the bolts of the double-leafed door of Horus' shrine, drawing them back and opening the door to reveal the divine statue within covered by a cloth. The priest uncovered the face of Horus, reciting, 'I have seen the God, and the Powerful One has seen me. The god rejoices at seeing me. I have gazed upon the statue of the Divine Winged Beetle, the sacred image of the Falcon of Gold.'[17] The ceremony of 'Seeing the God' was undoubtedly one of the most important rituals in the Service, for it marked the moment at which the essence of the God entered his statue, bringing it and the temple to life. Upon seeing the face of the god, the priest prostrated himself and kissed the ground. He then raised his arms in adoration of Horus before presenting him with myrrh. The myrrh symbolized a meal, the god's breakfast, but a selection of real food offerings had been laid out in the Hall of Offerings (*see* below).

Next came Horus' morning ablutions. The officiant 'laid hands on the God', in other words, lifted the statue out of its shrine. He then removed the cloth that had been draped over it the previous evening and touched the statue with unguent before presenting it with ritual cloths and purifying it with libations. The cloths were draped over the statue to become the robes worn during the day. There were four, in different colours — white, green, red and blue — and their presentation was interspersed with offerings of four balls of *bd*-natron (sodium carbonate), four balls of Upper Egyptian natron from El-Kab, and four balls of Lower Egyptian natron from Wadi Natrun. Then the statue was purified with water from ritual vases of red and green, after which it was lifted back into its shrine. Finally, with many censings, the Service came to an end. The doors of the shrine were closed once more and the officiant left the Sanctuary, walking backwards and brushing the sand with which the floor of the Sanctuary was covered in order to obliterate his footprints. Having walked round the Sanctuary censing it to restore its perfect purity, he closed its doors.

While the Morning Service was being performed for Horus, priests were visiting the chapels that open off the corridor surrounding the Sanctuary, and probably other parts of the temple also, to perform abbreviated versions of the rites being performed in the Sanctuary, thus bringing the whole temple to life for the day. Once this had been accomplished, a most important ritual, at least as far as members of the temple staff were concerned, was performed. The chief officiant proceeded to the Hall of Offerings (9) where he conducted special ceremonies for the benefit of the Royal Ancestors, including the presentation of the food offerings displayed in the Hall. Once this was accomplished, the priest recited the 'Reversion of Offerings', the ritual through which the divine recipients relinquished the offerings. They were then taken out of the temple through the same doors through which they had been brought in — the eastern doors (E and H) — 'to be distributed among the priests'.[18] The distribution was according to rank: the greater the rank the larger the share of offerings.

The inscriptions do not give many details about the Midday Service, which seems to have been very short. It may have consisted of libations alone being offered to the gods; but there are several inscriptions[19] that mention various kinds of bread, flowers, geese and grain being brought into the temple three times during the day. These, however, may have been used for other services. Clues to what these were are very few, but an inscription[20] on the east door of the Pronaos speaks of spells for lustrating the sacred images of Re 'in the twelve hours of the day'; and another[21] on a door-jamb in the Throne of Re (24) speaks of the priests who walk by to 'uncover the face of Him-of-pleasant-life (an epithet of Horus) from evening time without cease through the twelve (?) hours of the night, provisions held in their hands' which the gods and goddesses in Horus' train eat with him. These inscriptions seem to indicate that services were held at hourly intervals throughout the day and night.

The lack of importance seemingly attached to the Midday Service is consistent with the pattern of life in both ancient and modern Egypt, where breakfast was and is more important than the midday meal. The evening meal was more substantial, although the Evening Service, celebrated just before sunset, was a less elaborate version of the Morning Service. It took place not in the Sanctuary but in the Throne of Re (24). The God was prepared for the night by having his coloured cloths removed, after which he was 'put to bed' in his shrine. The doors of his shrine, and those of the Sanctuary, were closed, bolted and sealed; and Horus and his temple were left to sleep in safety until dawn next morning, when the whole procedure began again.

6 The Foundation and Consecration of Edfu Temple

In every temple a series of reliefs and inscriptions carved on the walls commemorated the laying of the foundations of the temple, which undoubtedly was carried out with elaborate cermonial. The reliefs, as was customary, show the King performing the rites: in this case, however, it was unlikely to be merely a conventional depiction but a record of the fact that the King in person did actually take part in the Foundation Ceremony.

Scenes recording the foundation of a temple are often linked to others concerned with the consecration of the building, a logical connection since the consecration must necessarily be preceded by the process of construction. The nucleus of a temple was usually dedicated as soon as it had been completed; and this dedication, together with the record of the temple's foundation, was commemorated in a series of scenes carved on the latest section to be built — in most cases, the hypostyle hall.

At Edfu, scenes depicting the various episodes in the Foundation Ceremony were carved on interior walls of both the Inner and Outer Hypostyle Halls and also on the exterior of the Enclosure Wall. The reason for having several sets of Foundation rituals is quite simple: the temple was built in different stages. The Naos was completed first, hence the Foundation scenes in the Inner Hypostyle Hall; and the Outer Hypostyle Hall, or Pronaos, was constructed sixteen years later, necessitating a recording within it of its own foundation. The building of the rest of the temple, including the Enclosure Wall, was completed later still and the Wall used for the depiction of the final Foundation Ceremony, which consists of fourteen scenes, read from south to north, carved on the first register of the outer face of the western Enclosure Wall.[1]

In the Inner Hypostyle Hall (5) scenes depicting the episodes of the Foundation Ceremony are arranged on the first registers of the east, west and south walls.[2] A central doorway in the south wall means that the scenes on this wall are arranged on either side of the opening, three on its left and three on its right. The subsequent scenes of the ritual follow alternately on the west and east walls of the Hall. This arrangement allowed the decorator to have a consecutive development of scenes depicting rites enacted first on behalf of Lower Egypt, on the west wall, followed by those enacted for Upper Egypt on the east wall. Where the titles of the officiating king are preserved, he bears, on the west wall, titles connected with

27   Pronaos, *Edfu Temple, interior: Foundation scene — 'King coming forth from the Palace'*

Lower Egypt, and, on the east wall, titles connected with Upper Egypt.

The first scene on either side of the doorway is the necessary preliminary to the ritual and shows the King emerging from his palace (**27**). Starting, according to 'rule', with the Lower Egyptian side (*see* p. 42), the scenes develop as follows: first scene to the left of the doorway followed by the first scene to its right; then the second to the left followed by the corresponding scene to the right; then the third scene to the left followed by the third scene to the right of the doorway. The remaining nine rites which make up the ritual are found in scenes on the west and east walls of the Hall. These scenes are read alternately from wall to wall while progressing along the register, starting with the scene at the southern end of the west wall, which is paralleled by a corresponding scene on the east wall.

In the Outer Hypostyle Hall (2) the eight scenes commemorating the foundation of the *Pronaos* are carved on the lowest registers of the south-west and west walls.[3] They are read along the register, starting with the two scenes on the south west wall and proceeding with the six scenes on the west wall. There is, however, a second set of Foundation scenes in the Outer Hypostyle Hall. These are on the first register of the north wall,[4] which is bisected by a doorway so that the wall is divided into two halves. The ten scenes which make up the Foundation Ceremony on this wall are divided equally between its two halves; and are read alternately from the left half of the wall to the right half, starting with the scene in

28   Pronaos, *Edfu Temple, interior: Foundation scene* — *'Measuring out the Foundations with Seshat'*

the north west corner of the Hall.

The Outer Hypostyle Hall was added to the original nucleus of the temple, which means that its northern wall was initially the south wall, or facade, of the *Naos*. The *Naos*, therefore, has two Foundation Ceremonies, one in the conventional place in the Inner Hypostyle Hall, the other on what was originally its facade. The explanation for these two sets of Foundation scenes may lie in the fact that after the first was carved — sometime between 212 and 206 BC, when the *Naos* was decorated — work on the temple was interrupted by disturbances in the Thebaïd, which lasted until the nineteenth year of the reign of Ptolemy V Epiphanes (186 BC). It may have been felt necessary to rededicate the temple, which at this time consisted of the *Naos* only, after the disturbances were settled, hence the second set of Foundation scenes on the *Naos*'s outer wall.

Several rites made up a Foundation Ceremony: lack of space sometimes necessitated that one or two be omitted from the record on the walls of the temple, but the whole repertoire would have been enacted during the performance of the Ceremony. The first ritual, which was carried out at night, was entitled 'Stretching the Cord'(**28**), whereby the building was oriented by aligning two stakes on a star: at Edfu, inscriptions in the temple tell us that it was oriented from Orion in the south to the Great Bear in the north. This was followed by the sacrifice of a goose, which had its throat cut before being placed in the foundation

29   Pronaos, Edfu Temple, interior: Foundation scene — 'Hacking up the Ground'

trench. In the second ritual, 'Releasing the Cord', the groundplan of the temple was marked out using four stakes and a length of gypsum-coated rope which was flicked so that traces of gypsum were left on the ground. Reliefs of these rituals show the King accompanied by Seshat, the goddess of writing and books, who in these scenes often appears in her form of Sefkhet-abwy (She-of-the-Seven-Horns) wearing on her head her characteristic head-dress of a pair of inverted horns over a star-like object.

The third ritual was entitled 'Hacking up the Ground'(**29**), that is, digging the foundation trenches of each wall of the temple. Reliefs of this ritual depict the King hacking the ground with a hoe. Next came 'Making the Bricks'. At Edfu the reliefs show the King making mud-bricks in a wooden mould in spite of the fact that from the Middle Kingdom at least temples had not been made of mud-brick but of stone. The fifth ritual was 'Scattering the Sand'(**30**), that is putting sand or pieces of broken pot at the bottom of the trench as a protection against water seepage.

The sixth ritual was 'Placing the Bricks'(**31**) and consisted of putting groups of objects at the corners of the foundation trenches. These so-called 'foundation deposits', which were intended to remain buried under the walls of the temple once they were erected, consisted of plaques of gold or faience inscribed with the name of the King in whose reign the temple was built, and small samples of the materials that were used in the building: small blocks of sandstone, plaques of

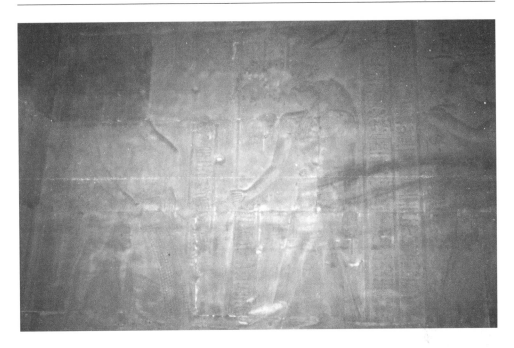

30   Pronaos, Edfu Temple, interior: Foundation scene — 'Scattering the Sand'

31   Pronaos, Edfu Temple, interior: Foundation scene — 'Placing the Bricks'

silver and bronze, pieces of alabaster, lapis lazuli, carnelian and turquoise, and small amounts of resin and clay, together with bowls and other containers. The foundation deposits often included miniature models of the tools used in the construction of the temple — wooden hoes, copper adzes and chisels, bronze knives — and baskets.

The seventh ritual was entitled 'Scattering *besen*'— *besen* was probably chalk, which the King poured from a small container into the foundations in order to purify them. After this purification, the Foundation Ceremony was concluded with 'Making Offerings', notably of geese and bulls' heads. Only after the Foundation Ceremony had been completed could work begin on the building of the temple.

The first festival ever to be celebrated in Edfu or indeed any other temple was that in which the new building was consecrated. This ceremony, which was called 'Handing over the House to its Lord', was basically a mixture of the Daily Ritual and the Opening of the Mouth Ceremony (*see* below); and the traditional time for it to take place was either on New Year's Day,[5] or on New Year's Eve,[6] with an annual re-dedication ceremony celebrated probably on New Year's Day. At Edfu, the texts describing the consecration of the temple are engraved on the frieze on the exterior of the east and west walls of the Outer Hypostyle Hall.[7] According to the usual 'rule', one might have expected the ceremonies recorded on the west wall to be those celebrated for Lower Egypt and those on the east for Upper Egypt; but in fact this is not so. The east wall is dedicated solely to rituals peculiar to the Opening of the Mouth Ceremony, the west wall to rites carried out during the Daily Ritual, some of which were also performed during the Opening of the Mouth. The two sets of texts complement, and were presumably used in conjunction with, each other. The Consecration Ceremony texts engraved on the exterior of Edfu's Outer Hypostyle Hall seem to be based on a very much abbreviated directory of the rituals deemed essential to the performance of the Ceremony. The formulae normally recited during the performance are omitted from the inscriptions, and only the titles of the rites are given.

The Opening of the Mouth Ceremony was an ancient ritual that was performed upon the body of a deceased person to reanimate the life force, enabling him, or her, to 'live' in the Afterlife with the full use of his mouth to speak, eat and drink. It was also performed on statues and reliefs in temples and tombs, for the ancient Egyptians believed that divinities and the dead could only become immanent in any reliefs and statues that depicted them after these inanimate objects had been imbued with life through the performance of the Opening of the Mouth.

There were over a hundred episodes in a full Opening of the Mouth Ceremony, including many forms of lustration, censing and anointing with perfumes and unguents, and the sacrifice of animals and birds. In one episode the right foreleg of a living ox calf was amputated and pointed towards the beneficiary of the Ceremony. The hieroglyph depicting the foreleg denoted strength, and perhaps it was considered that the act of presenting the foreleg of the still-living animal transferred the life force of the unfortunate calf to the recipient of the Opening of the Mouth. The most important episodes involved touching the mouth, and other parts of the body, with various ritual implements, notably a ceremonial adze (*see* below), while reciting formulae such as 'I perform the Opening of the Mouth upon this your mouth so that you may speak in the Afterlife' or 'I perform the Opening of the Mouth upon these your eyes so that you may see in the Afterlife'.

An adze, which was an arched metal blade fastened across the top of a wooden handle with leather thongs, was an ancient Egyptian woodworking tool. A ceremonial adze was made from the so-called 'metal of heaven' (*bi3 n pt*), in other words, meteoritic iron, which was obtained from meteorites that had fallen in the desert. It was comparatively rare and the only iron known to the Egyptians until the telluric metal was imported from the Near East in the New Kingdom. Because of its perceived divine origin and its rarity meteoritic iron was used only to fashion ritual implements. The adze used in the Opening of the Mouth Ceremony mimicked the creative process of carving and sculpture, and it was perhaps thought that in so doing the finishing touches were being put to the 'new creation'.

Before the Consecration Ceremony began at Edfu, the statues of Horus and the co-templar deities were gathered together, probably in the Outer Hypostyle Hall, where the chief rites of the Daily Ritual were carried out: each statue was anointed, censed, offered libations and presented with pellets of incense and natron to purify its mouth, arrayed with a headcloth and four coloured cloths and presented with its insignia. Then eight rituals from the Opening of the Mouth Ceremony were performed on the statues. In the first, an officiant impersonating the god Ptah opened the mouths of the statues with a copper chisel, and an officiant impersonating Sokar opened their eyes. The next rite, entitled 'Taking the Sorcerer', the Sorcerer (*wr-kh3w*) being a wavy wand or rod topped by a ram's head, was followed by 'Presenting the Finger of Fine Gold' and 'Offering the Copper Adze of Anubis'. The fifth rite, entitled 'Ushering in the Courtiers (*smrw*)', was one in which the eyes of the statues were opened with adzes and their mouths touched with four small slabs of stone (*'bwt*). Courtiers are not known to have fulfilled this function in any other version of Opening the Mouth, and so it is probable that *smrw* in the inscription was wrongly written in error for *s3-mry-f,* the title (son-whom-he-loves) borne by the officiant who normally carried out this act.

Next came three rituals in which animals were killed — in the first a goose and a goat were decapitated, in the second a male ox from Upper Egypt was slaughtered, and in the third long-horned cattle were butchered and geese had their necks wrung. The enactment of these rituals was probably symbolic, the actual slaughter of the animals having taken place previously in preparation for setting out before the statues a 'repast of bread, meat and beer', after which the statues were returned to the places reserved for them throughout the temple.

The meal was normally the culmination of both the Opening of the Mouth

Ceremony and the Daily Ritual, but in the Consecration Ceremony it was followed by a second, extensive, Opening of the Mouth in which priests worked their way through each hall and chapel in the temple performing the rite on the reliefs and scenes on the walls. This had the effect of bringing the temple to life by allowing the divinities whose forms were depicted on the walls to become immanent at will in the reliefs, a magical ability that was extended to the inanimate objects that were depicted, allowing them to become the actual equivalents of the food and drink, the floral offerings and the various types of vessel that they represented.

The Consecration Ceremony ended with a special meal held in honour of the priests and the craftsmen who had built the temple. The relevant inscription on the eastern frieze of the Outer Hypostyle Hall states that it was Sokar who fed the priesthood from the oblation of bread, meat and beer, which means, presumably, that the officiant who had impersonated the god during the Ceremony was responsible for regaling the priests with food and drink. The corresponding inscription on the western frieze records that the craftsmen also were entertained in the same manner. Although priests normally received payment in kind through the 'reversion of offerings' (*see* p. 84) at the end of the Daily Ritual, for example, the Edfu text is the only known allusion to the custom of giving a meal to craftsmen after they had finished building a temple, a practice often observed today in topping out, the traditional drinking ceremony held in celebration of the completion of a building.

Once the meal was ended, the temple was 'handed over to its lord', in theory by the King in person. The building was now complete, it had been consecrated, and it was ready for the services and festivals that were celebrated throughout the year in the House of Horus. These were of two kinds: the services that were performed every day as the Daily Ritual; and the calendar feasts, great festivals of varying lengths that were observed on certain dates throughout the year. The activities in the temple reflected the belief that it was the house, or home, of Horus; thus the Daily Ritual mimiced day to day domestic affairs, which were enlivened by occasional high days and holidays — the annual festivals. The Daily Ritual was always celebrated privately within the temple by a small, select number of priests; the annual festivals, on the other hand, all involved great processions of divine statues accompanied by large numbers of priests. Some processions took place within the temple, from which members of the public were excluded, others within the temple enclosure, to which certain privileged laypeople were admitted. Sometimes the statue of the deity of one temple was taken to visit another in his or her own temple and on these occasions the general public not only witnessed the procession but took part in it in a party atmosphere.

7 The New Year Festival

Special festivals were celebrated in temples during the course of a single year. Two calendars[1] listing the festivals observed at Edfu, although incompletely preserved, show that there were over forty and that they varied in length from between one and fifteen days, with the average calendar feast being five days long. In most cases, the Edfu calendars list only the names of the festivals and tell us little about their nature or how they were celebrated. In addition, there are surprising omissions from the lists, notably any reference to the special festivals that were celebrated for Osiris throughout Egypt during the Fourth Month of the Inundation Season. At Edfu, there were three rooms dedicated to the cult of Osiris (*see* p. 72), with a selection from the text of the Osiris Mysteries carved on their walls. There are also claims that the Leg of Osiris was kept in the temple, and that he was mummified at Edfu.[2] It is unlikely, therefore, that festivals of Osiris were not celebrated at Edfu, but apart from references to the Festival of Sokar on the 26th day of the Fourth Month of Inundation,[3] they are ignored in the calendars. Only four of the annual festivals can be reconstructed with any accuracy — the New Year Festival, the Coronation of the Sacred Falcon, the Feast of the Joyous Union and the Festival of Victory — and these four great festivals will be discussed in this and the following chapters.

The New Year Festival

In ancient Egypt, the civil year began on the day that the annual rising of the Nile at Memphis was expected to start, that is, on the first day of the Inundation Season, which was the nineteenth day of July (in the Julian calendar) when the civil and astronomical calendars (*see* Glossary) were in step. At Edfu, the New Year Festival commenced on the thirtieth day of the Fourth Month of Summer, that is, on the last day of the old calendar year, continued over the five epagomenal days (*see* Glossary), and may have ended on the fifth day of the First Month of Inundation. However, the calendar entries for the fourth and fifth days of that month make no reference to the New Year, instead naming the fourth day *The Festival of the Behdetite,*[4] and the fifth day *The Festival of Horus of Behdet* which would seem to suggest that at Edfu the New Year Festival proper lasted for nine rather than eleven days. The texts give little information about the rituals enacted on the days before and after New Year's Day, and concentrate on the Day itself.

The New Year Festival was primarily concerned with the renewal of life and fertility for the people of Egypt, for the land itself, for its gods and above all for the King upon whose well-being the prosperity of Egypt depended. At Edfu, this renewal was symbolized by the rays of the sun falling upon a statue of Horus as the sun-god, Re-Horakhty. To this end the rooms within the temple called the Pure Place (14), with its ceiling decorated with reliefs depicting the sun traversing the sky during the twelve hours of the day, and the Food Altar (13), which was open to the sky, the stairways leading to and from the roof, and the Place of the First Feast, the name by which the small pavilion on the roof was known, were all specially designed to facilitate this all-important event.

At the heart of the New Year Festival were the ceremonies carried out on the first day of the Inundation Season, New Year's Day. Before dawn on this day, the King or his deputy, accompanied by the senior priests of the temple, by-passed the Sanctuary, normally the first area of the temple to be opened for the Daily Ritual, and entered the Mesen Room (16) behind it, where stood two portable shrines containing statues of Horus and Hathor. Here he performed the opening rites of the Daily Ritual: mounting the steps of each *naos* in turn, opening its doors to reveal the statue within it, and performing a brief adoration. The shrine of each god was then placed upon a rectangular gilded platform surmounted by a canopy set on four pillars and having a metal ring at its four corners. Throughout the ceremonies of the day, each of these assemblages was carried in procession by eight priests, who supported it on their hands and steadied it by means of cords passed round their necks and then threaded through the metal rings at the corners of the platform. These priests, who were called the Companions, impersonated the Four Sons of Horus, the minor deities who guarded the contents of the canopic jars in which the viscera of the dead were placed, and the four sons of Mekhentenirty, a form of Horus whose name means 'Face-without-Eyes'. A ninth priest, who acted as a coordinator, represented Mekhentenirty himself.

The shrines having been set on their platforms, the procession formed into two files and, with the Sacred Lance of Horus preceding his shrine, and the Lance of Khonsu set before that of Hathor, made its way along the narrow corridor to the east of the Sanctuary to the Food Altar (13) and thence up a short flight of steps to the Pure Place (14) leading off it. The divine statues were set down in the Pure Place facing south so that they could look upon the piles of offerings theoretically assembled in the Food Altar below, details of which are pictured in reliefs on the room's south and east walls. Five lines of inscription on the south wall list the offerings: bread, beer, wine, milk, honey, geese, poultry and meat, together with flowers, perfumes and unguents. At this point, Horus and Hathor were joined by the statues of the co-templar deities, who were assembled in the Food Altar facing the south wall so that they too could 'read' the menu of offerings. By this time, the Food Altar and the Pure Place would have been full of shrines and priests, with no space left for real offerings: but altars throughout the rest of the temple, above all in the Court of Offerings, or Forecourt (1),[5] were piled high with a wide variety of food and drink.

The divine statues were unveiled, the toilet episodes of the Daily Ritual were carried out to the accompaniment of special hymns, and crowns and cloths were presented. Scenes carved on the east and west walls of the Pure Place show the reigning sovereigns and their parents together with the statues of their predecessors, for according to instructions laid down in the Decree of Canopus, issued in 238 BC, the Royal Ancestors played a prominent part in the New Year Festival. After these rites had been carried out, the procession re-formed in order to make its way to the roof of the temple. It progressed from the Food Altar to the Central Hall (11) and then to the Hall of Offerings (9) where it turned left through the door (F) onto the winding eastern stairway that leads up to the roof.

At this point the original procession was divided into two files, one escorting Horus' portable shrine, the other escorting Hathor's. The composition of Horus' file, which was essentially the same as Hathor's, consisted of a leading group of priests, probably fifteen in number, carrying the sacred standards, and securing the safety of the shrine's passage by purifying the route, so driving evil away from the god. Behind them came more priests, some wearing masks in order to impersonate divinities, carrying food, drink, offerings and clothing. Next came the immediate escort of the deity, led by a reader-priest: the senior priests of the temple, carrying incense, libations, semi-precious stones and clothing, with the High Priest behind them. Immediately behind the High Priest marched a man dressed in royal regalia and carrying the Sacred Lance of Horus. Next came the King and Queen, bare footed, the King burning incense and the Queen shaking rattles, both looking over their shoulders at the portable shrine of Horus, still carried by the nine Companions, which was immediately behind them. Behind Horus' shrine were yet more priests, each carrying one of the co-templar divinities in a portable shrine. A fan bearer brought up the rear of the procession.

The main part of the ceremony took place on the roof of the temple, presumably in the Place of the First Feast. This chapel, long since disappeared from Edfu, was probably similar to the one at Denderah (32): a stone pavilion with the spaces between its columns filled with screen walls to half column height, allowing the interior of the chapel to be flooded with light during the day. The statue of Horus was placed in the chapel, flanked by the statues of Hathor and the other deities, all facing south and all veiled. The Daily Ritual was repeated and then, at mid-day, the veil was removed from the face of Horus, allowing the rays of the sun to fall upon it, thus symbolizing the mystic union of the sun with the god, the culmination of the New Year Festival. It was probably at this point that the annual re-dedication of the temple took place, although the texts make no reference to it.

The fertility and well-being of Egypt having been assured, and the life and potency of the temple and the gods within it renewed, the ceremonies on the roof concluded. The procession re-formed and, leaving the roof via the western stairway, made its way down through the hypostyle halls into the Forecourt. There, a roll call of the administrative districts (*see* Glossary under 'nome') of Upper and Lower Egypt was made, beginning with the First District of Lower

32   *Roof Chapel, Denderah Temple*

Egypt (Memphis), followed by the First District of Upper Egypt (Elephantine). This re-dedication of Egypt, district by district, was carried out in the presence of certain privileged people, such as the local mayor and his counterparts from other towns and cities. The preceding ceremonies, however, were enacted behind the closed doors of the temple, hidden from the view of the general public whose welfare they were supposed to guarantee.

8 The Installation of the Sacred Falcon

The Installation of the Sacred Falcon at Edfu was at heart a coronation ceremony in which a living falcon, rather than a human king, was crowned. The falcon represented Horus, the royal god *par excellence*, for a reigning king was regarded as the living Horus, the earthly representation of Horus son of Osiris; and it was the protagonist in the great festival celebrated each year to reaffirm the principle of kingship. The festival was celebrated on the first five days of the First Month of Winter (the fifth month of the Egyptian year). The date is significant, for the great Osiris festivals were celebrated in the last month of the previous season, the final day of which marked Osiris' resurrection as a dead king restored to a semblance of life before being buried. On the following day, that is, the first day of the First Month of Winter, his son Horus assumed the crown, setting a precedent for his successors as Kings of Egypt, for whom the first day of the First Month of Winter became the conventional date of their accession. Throughout the Installation of the Sacred Falcon there was complete identity between the Sacred Falcon and the King; thus the festival was more than the annual selection and crowning of a sacred bird, it was also the means by which the King renewed the powers conferred upon him at his own coronation.

The Installation of the Sacred Falcon is recorded in a magnificent set of reliefs carved on the first two registers of the inner face of the northern Enclosure Wall of the temple.[1] At the top of the wall, exactly in the middle, a winged disk marks the axis of the temple: the eight major scenes that record the principal rites in the Installation, four on each register, are arranged in groups of two on either side of the axis, with each of the four outermost scenes supplemented by smaller subsidiary scenes. In the scenes on the eastern half of the wall the king wears the Red Crown of Lower Egypt, in those on the western half he wears the White Crown of Upper Egypt. The royal *cartouches* in most scenes are empty, perhaps because at the time when they were carved (around 88 BC) there was some doubt about the outcome of the struggle for power between Ptolemy IX Soter II and his brother Ptolemy X Alexander I (*see* p. 27). Observing the rules that the reading of scenes usually begins with those on the lowest register on a wall and that rites were performed first for Lower Egypt, then for Upper Egypt (*see* p. 43), the ritual opens with the two reliefs at the easternmost end of the lowest register, followed by the corresponding reliefs on the west, followed by the relief immediately to the east of the axis, followed by that to its west. The procedure is then repeated with the second register.

The reliefs by themselves would not be sufficient to reconstruct the many episodes in the Installation of the Sacred Falcon: but they are accompanied by long hieroglyphic texts that enable us to do so; and are amplified by inscriptions in other areas of the temple, notably on the Pylon Gateway (*see* below), and in a hieroglyphic summary of the whole festival.[2] It seems that on the morning of the first day of the festival, the statue of Horus of Behdet was taken from its shrine in the Sanctuary (15) and placed on a litter. The litter was carried by six priests representing the ancestors, that is, the kings who had once ruled Nekhen (Hierakonpolis) in Upper Egypt and Pe (Buto) in the Delta, the predynastic kingdoms of Egypt. The three priests manning the carrying poles at the rear of the litter wore jackal masks, the three at the front falcon masks: they are referred to as the Souls of Pe and Nekhen (**colour plate 12**). Significantly, the litter was not the one usually used for transporting the statue of Horus, which was a processional bark designed to display the god, as its ancient Egyptian name implies (*wṯs-nfrw*: literally 'displaying (*wṯs*) beauty (*nfrw*)'), but the type that was depicted in traditional scenes of the coronation of a human king.

The litter was carried in a procession that was probably very similar to that of the New Year Festival (*see* p. 94): at the front came priests bearing the standards, followed by senior members of the priesthood; priests carrying the statues of the co-templar deities in their portable shrines brought up the rear of the procession. Directly in front of the litter was the King, his head turned round so that he faced the God as he walked, burning incense to purify the way. The text makes the point that the procession observed complete silence, 'no man speaking to his fellow'.[3] It made its way out of the temple through the great doors of the Pylon Gateway and proceeded *via* the south gate of the *temenos* (*see* Glossary) to the Temple of the Sacred Falcon. This temple has disappeared but it was probably to the east of the *Mammisi*. The portable shrines of the co-templar deities were assembled in front of the Temple of the Sacred Falcon, and the litter bearing Horus was set down facing them: the time for the selection of the new Sacred Falcon had arrived.

The selection of the Sacred Falcon is not actually depicted in the reliefs; but the hieroglyphic summary of the festival (*see* above) refers to it. The choice was made by Horus of Behdet and the method of selection was oracular, the litter bearing the statue of the god probably moving forward to answer 'yes', and moving back a pace to indicate 'no'. The names of 'the high priests, the priests and the great officials were called, one by one, so that His Majesty might choose one of them'.[4] All were rejected. The procession then moved into the so-called broad hall (*wsḫt*) — which was either the Forecourt or the Hypostyle Hall — of the Temple of the Sacred Falcon where the god took up his position 'standing in between the gate', in other words, at the entrance to the hall.[5] At this point, a number of falcons were brought into the temple to be paraded before Horus of Behdet. These birds had been reared in a special area of the precinct of Edfu Temple expressly to provide one suitable for Horus of Behdet to select as that year's sacred falcon. We do not

33   North Enclosure Wall, Edfu Temple: the Sacred Falcon sitting before Horus of Behdet during the Installation of the Sacred Falcon

know the criteria used but presumably the chosen falcon was the largest, strongest, most handsome bird; and it was recognized by the god as his heir, the chosen king for the coming year.

Once the Sacred Falcon had been selected, it was placed in front of Horus in his litter (**33**) and carried into the Temple of Horus for the Ceremony of Recognition. From the Forecourt (1), the procession entered the door in the rear wall of the south-eastern colonnade and climbed to the roof of the bridge between the two wings of the Pylon Gateway. This bridge was called the *Balcony of the Falcon*[6] and the *Window of Appearances;*[7] and inscriptions carved on the side walls of the east and west wings of the Pylon Gateway above the monumental gateway[8] make it clear that this was the place from which Horus displayed his heir, the newly-chosen Sacred Falcon, to 'the people'. Who 'the people' were we do not know, but presumably priests and certain privileged laymen stood in the Forecourt, while members of the public gathered in front of the Pylon Gateway.

After the Sacred Falcon had been acclaimed, the procession descended from the balcony and made its way into the temple, probably to the Great Hall (5), where the actual Coronation was performed. At the beginning of the ceremony, the living falcon was placed upon a rectangular block of stone set under a light canopy. The stone was carved in imitation of a *serekh*, the oblong frame, carved at the bottom with a design depicting the panelled facade of a royal palace, inside which it had been the custom during the first three dynasties of Egyptian history to record the chief name, the so-called Horus name, of the king. Just as a *serekh* was surmounted with the figure of a falcon - the god, Horus — so the Sacred Falcon perched atop its elaborately carved block of stone, ready to be anointed king (**34**). It was then presented with a ceremonial collar, a Symbol of Eternity (**35**) and four bouquets. The first bouquet was called the Posy of Horus of Behdet; and the inscriptions make it clear that in conferring this Posy the King bestowed upon the Sacred Falcon not only protection, sovereignty, wealth, good health and a long lifetime but also the appurtenances of several deities — the Two-feather Crown of Amun, the diadem of Re, the regalia of Kamutef and the kingly office of Atum. The second bouquet to be presented, the Posy of Re, also bestowed upon the recipient more than flowers. By means of this Posy the Sacred Falcon received sovereignty, endurance and a long lifetime; and above all the Double Crown. The third Posy, that of Hathor, brought love, long life and health; and protection from enemies. The fourth Posy, that of Atum, conferred fertility and prosperity.

For the second part of the Coronation Ceremony the living falcon was placed on a seat set on the back of the figure of a lion, with the statue of Horus of Behdet, also set on a lion, standing protectively behind it (**36**). To the accompaniment of two long hymns,[9] one of which, the Litany of Sekhmet, was sung to ensure the protection of the Sacred Falcon, and the other, the Litany of the Happy Year, sung to greet the new regnal year that was being inaugurated, the Sacred Falcon was presented with the royal insignia and with numerous amulets. His beak was touched with milk. Finally, invocations were made to ensure the protection, by day and by night to the end of eternity, not just of the god's temple and everything

34   *North Enclosure Wall, Edfu Temple: the Sacred Falcon seated upon a* serekh-*shaped stone during the Installation of the Sacred Falcon*

35   *North Enclosure Wall, Edfu Temple: the Sacred Falcon being presented with the symbol of eternity during the Installation of the Sacred Falcon*

*36   North Enclosure Wall, Edfu Temple: the Sacred Falcon and Horus of Behdet seated
upon lion-shaped chairs during the Installation of the Sacred Falcon*

in it, but more importantly of the Sacred Falcon himself, together with Horus of
Behdet and the living King, for all three were considered as one.

The Coronation Ceremony completed, it was time for the final phase in the
Installation of the Sacred Falcon. This took place in the Sacred Falcon's own
temple, where an elaborate Grace before Meat[10] was sung before the King
presented the Falcon with choice pieces of meat, the flesh symbolizing the
destroyed enemies of both god and king. Lastly came the Banquet, which is
indicated by a scene entitled *Burning myrrh: bringing the god to his meat* in which the
Sacred Falcon is told 'the scent of myrrh is for your nose, it fills your nostrils so
that your heart may receive the portions of meat on its scent'.[11] As in the Daily
Service, the offering of myrrh symbolized an actual meal. At the end of the
Banquet, Horus of Behdet was carried back to the Sanctuary in the main temple
leaving the newly installed falcon in possession of the Temple of the Sacred
Falcon.

The hieroglyphic summary of the festival makes it clear that at the end of the
day's proceedings there was a prolonged bout of feasting and merrymaking 'by all
the people of this city. Making festival.[12] Repeating festivity. Celebrating the feast
by men and women until the completion of the first day of this festival which is
called the royal coronation, this festival which is celebrated year by year.'[13] The
festival had another four days to run but the texts give no information about what

happened on them. There was no necessity to select the Sacred Falcon again, but the rituals of purification and protection, and those closely connected with the coronation, were probably repeated every day. The feasting certainly was.

It may seem strange that so much effort was put into the coronation of a bird. In trying to explain the undoubted importance that was attached to the Installation of the Sacred Falcon it should be remembered that since the Persian conquest of 525 BC, Egypt had been ruled by foreigners. Despite the fact that the Ptolemies adopted Pharaonic titles and patronized the ancient Egyptian religion, they were regarded as usurpers by the natives of the Thebaïd, of which Edfu was one of the most important towns, who rejected Hellenization and clung steadfastly to the old way of life and to old religious practices. One can sympathize with the view expressed by the eminent English Egyptologist, Aylward Blackman (1883-1956), who considered that the patriotic priesthood of a great Upper Egyptian temple such as Edfu:

> may well have been more ready to assign the sovereignty over their country to their sacred bird, which, like the Pharaoh of old, was the embodiment of Horus, than to their Macedonian rulers seated in the utterly alien city of Alexandria.[14]

9 The Feast of the Joyous Union

The Feast of the Joyous Union[1] celebrated the sacred marriage between Horus of Edfu and the goddess Hathor of Denderah. It was a popular festival in that an unusually large proportion of its rites took place outwith the temple, allowing the population at large to witness them. Thus it was of interest to, and in varying degree involved, not just the people of Edfu but the whole of Upper Egypt at least, from Elephantine (modern Aswan) in the south to Denderah in the north.

The Feast was celebrated at Edfu in the Third Month of Summer (the eleventh month of the ancient Egyptian year), beginning on the day of the New Moon and ending fifteen days later on the day of the Full Moon. At the time when the inscriptions describing the Feast were engraved on the walls of Edfu's Forecourt (*see* p. 62) the Third Month of Summer would have corresponded to mid-July to mid-August in our calendar; but, since the date of the Feast was governed by the lunar month, the exact days within the civil calendar on which it was celebrated varied slightly from year to year according to the phases of the moon.

The preliminary ceremonies began at Denderah fourteen days before the New Moon,[2] when the statue of Hathor was carried out of her temple to begin the journey to Edfu. Accompanied by elaborate ceremonies, including the symbolic offering of the first fruits of the fields, the statue of the divine bride was installed in Hathor's magnificent state barge which was then slowly towed upstream. The barge and its tow-boats were joined by other craft carrying priests, the Mayor and other dignitaries of the town of Denderah and large numbers of pilgrims. During the voyage to Edfu, Hathor made visits to the temples of other deities: the inscriptions mention that at Thebes (Luxor) her statue was carried ashore to pay a state visit to the goddess Mut of Asheru at Karnak; and that stops were made at Pi-mer (modern Komir) some 45 miles (70km) south of Thebes (Luxor) and at Hierakonpolis, opposite the modern El-Kab, about 10 miles (16km) north of Edfu. The fact that the journey between Denderah and Edfu, a distance of only about 110 miles (180km), took fourteen days to complete would seem to indicate that stops were made at other places also, although they are not mentioned in the inscriptions. From every town and village along the route more and more pilgrims, including the mayors of Pi-mer and Hierakonpolis and their entourages, joined the flotilla The priests of Hierakonpolis brought with them the statue of the local form of Horus. The banks of the Nile must have been thronged with people watching Hathor's glittering progress and revelling in what was a time of peace and happiness, when even 'the crocodiles in the Nile were so quiescent that they did not dart up to attack'.[3]

Eventually, in mid-afternoon of the Day of the New Moon, Hathor, accompanied by what must by then have been a very large fleet of ships of all sizes, arrived at Edfu. She was greeted at the quayside by the statue of Horus accompanied by his entourage and by the mayor of Elephantine and yet more pilgrims. The statues of the two deities were taken to a nearby shrine where various ceremonies were performed, the most important of which was the Opening of the Mouth (*see* p. 90) and which included the offering of the first fruits of the field, the presentation of the field, driving the calves (*see* p. 110), offering Maat (*see* p. 52) and making numerous offerings of food. When these rites had been completed, the statues of Horus and Hathor were placed aboard their respective boats and, accompanied by the Mayors of Komir, Hierakonpolis and Elephantine and throngs of pilgrims, proceeded along a canal which led from the riverside to a landing-stage close by the Temple of Horus. On the way, the procession halted at a place called the Mound of Geb where the Opening of the Mouth was performed again, the appropriate rituals celebrated and yet more offerings made.

Finally, the procession arrived at the landing-stage, which was probably just outside a door in the east *temenos* wall of the temple. There, Horus and his bride disembarked and made their way into the temple via the door (B) in the south-eastern corner of the Forecourt. Inscriptions on the door jambs record the hymns of welcome that were chanted for the goddess who was mistress of intoxication, of song and of myrrh, the mistress of virgins who provided husbands for her favourites. What happened next we do not know. It is probable that there was no actual marriage ceremony, since such a ceremony was not customary in ancient Egypt;[4] and also probable that Horus and Hathor spent their wedding night in the *Mammisi*.

The citizens of Edfu and the devotees of Hathor who had come from far and wide were treated to a night of feasting and drinking. Countless provisions were made freely available by the temple staff and the inscriptions record the details:

> There are all kinds of bread in loaves numerous as grains of sand. Oxen abound like locusts. The smell of roast fowl, gazelle, oryx and ibex reaches the sky. Wine flows freely throughout the town like the Nile Flood bursting forth from the Two Caverns. Myrrh scattered on the brazier with incense can be smelled a mile away. The city is bestrewn with faience, glittering with natron and garlanded with flowers and fresh herbs. Its youths are drunk, its citizens are glad, its young maidens are beautiful to behold; rejoicing is all around it and festivity is in all its quarters. There is no sleep to be had in it until dawn.[5]

When dawn came on the second day of the Feast the festival underwent a change of emphasis. There is no more mention of a sacred marriage, even though the child of Horus and Hathor was said to have been conceived on the fourth night. Instead, the inscriptions refer to the Festival of Behdet. On the morning after the wedding night, that is, the first day of the Festival of Behdet, Horus and Hathor were taken in a great procession across the desert to the burial ground of Behdet, which seems to have been some distance to the west, or possibly the south-west. The procession was preceded by the five sacred lances and the statues of Horus and Hathor were accompanied by those of the visiting deities. They were escorted by priests and town dignitaries, and by large numbers of the citizens of Edfu and Denderah and of pilgrims from far afield.

The burial ground of Behdet, which contained at least four burial mounds identified as those of the divine ancestors, the ancient gods of Edfu, was within a sacred grove of trees. At its edge was an enclosure known as the Upper Temple. It is probable that every temple necropolis of the Ptolemaic Period contained a sacred grove; certainly, all the principal centres of Osiris worship did, especially the Abaton on the island of Philae at Elephantine (modern Aswan), U-peker at Abydos, and Busiris in the Delta. The ceremonies performed at Edfu's Upper Temple have very close parallels with the rites of the Osiris Mysteries celebrated at the Abaton, a similarity that provides a clue to the real significance of the Festival of Behdet.

At the First Mound, special hymns were chanted and the priests made offerings to the ancestors on behalf of Horus and Hathor. The offerings consisted of bread, beer, bulls, birds and 'every good thing', and after they were made the ceremony of treading the grave was enacted. Once the rites had been performed, a period of merrymaking ensued; and then the procession re-formed and made its way down from the Upper Temple to a hall in the House of Life (*see* p. 50). There a series of special rites was performed, chief amongst them the slaughter of an ox and a goat, both red, considered an unlucky colour because of its association with Seth, followed by the despatch to the four compass points of four geese, each carrying the message that Horus of Behdet had taken possession of the White Crown of Upper Egypt and the Red Crown of Lower Egypt. Then arrows were shot to the south, north, west and east by a priest called *s3-mry.f* or 'the Beloved Son', who represented Horus the son of Osiris, for whom he conducted the burial rites.

The subsequent rites were of a prophylactic nature. A red wax model of a hippopotamus, with the names of the King's enemies inscribed on it, was brought in. The names of these enemies were then written on a sheet of new papyrus; and a hippopotamus was modelled in sand. And then, according to the texts, 'every harmful thing that you can think of was done to them'[6]. Next came 'the trampling of the fishes' wherein the enemies of the King personified as fish were trodden on; and finally the King, or his representative, smote his foes with a sword. An explanation of these prophylactic rites was addressed to the public, who were told that the hippopotamus and the fishes were symbols of the King's enemies who by these means had been destroyed, an indication that the rites had probably been performed in sight of the general public in order to demonstrate that the magical protection of the King and, through him, of Egypt and its people, had been carried out successfully.

The ceremonies of the first day of the Festival of Behdet came to an end in the evening with the drinking of beer and wine in the presence of the gods, after which they retired for the night to the Birth House and their devotees spent another night making merry.

The second, third and fourth days of the Festival were a repeat of the first, except that the rites enacted at the Upper Temple took place at a different burial mound each day. The events of days five to thirteen day are unclear. One set of inscriptions states that on these days the gods were taken in procession to the burial ground, but another indicates that the procession took place only on the first four days, after which the gods did not leave the temple. A likely explanation is that the ceremonies of the fifth and subsequent days were on a much reduced scale compared to those on the first four days. Finally, on the fourteenth day of the Festival of Behdet, Hathor left for home. Her statue was taken out of the Birth Temple and, accompanied by Horus, it was taken by canal to the quay on the Nile. There the Opening of the Mouth, the treading on the grave and other rites were carried out, and then, after the hymn to the Sacred Harpoon of Horus had been recited, Hathor boarded her boat and was towed northwards to Denderah.

It is clear from the episodes outlined above that the Feast of the Joyous Union fell into two distinct parts: the rituals celebrated on the afternoon and evening of the day of the New Moon; and those celebrated on the following fourteen days as the Festival of Behdet. The Festival of Behdet itself seems to have fallen into two unequal periods of four and ten days. The purpose of the first day's ceremonies is clearly to do with the sacred marriage between Horus and Hathor; but equally clearly those of the Festival of Behdet are concerned with the worship of the demi-gods known as the Ancestors, the Divine Souls of Edfu for whom Horus and Hathor acted as mortuary priests.

There are a number of inscriptions throughout the temple [7] that contain information about the Ancestors. They were nine in number, and they were giants — the mummy of the eldest of them, Ba-neb-Djedet, was said to be thirty-six cubits (approximately 75 feet) tall! Apart from Ba-neb-Djedet, whose name means *the ram who is lord of Djedet,* a town in the Western Delta where the soul of Osiris was worshipped in the form of a sacred ram, there were Hor-shefy (Horus the ram-headed), Menhi-wer (the Great Butcher), Hor-shedet (Horus of the Fayum, known as Krokodilopolis in the Ptolemaic Period), Neteraa-em-sepetef (The Great God in his Province), Neb-shennu (The Lord of Trees), Bennu (the divine Phoenix), Henty-Behdet (The One who is pre-eminent in Behdet) and Neb-Hoot-Waret (The Lord of Hoot-Waret i.e. the Mansion of the Leg (of Osiris), known to the Greeks as Avaris). They were said to have been born in Hesret, the necropolis of Khemenu (el-Eshmunein) in Upper Egypt; and to have come forth from Neref, the necropolis of Henen-nesut (Herakleopolis), just south of the Fayum, and entered Upper Egyptian Behdet.

Most of the inscriptions concerning the Ancestors are found in scenes depicting the burning of incense or the pouring of libations, the incense symbolizing food, the libations the giving of life and strength. In one such scene of offering incense and libation, which occurs on the eastern exterior wall of the Naos, it is said of the Divine Souls that they were

> the children of the Sun God, Re, who created them before heaven or earth existed, before a penis emitted its seed or an invigorated limb moved. They came with Re from the High Hill having been born in Wenu and nursed in the Pomegranate-tree Province. They journeyed through the Two Lands (Egypt) and crossed the river (Nile) to reach Behdet (Edfu) in order to conceal their bodies beside the great golden Winged Beetle (Horus). They ascended to the sky from Throne-of-Re (Edfu), and having crossed the desert with the God-with-the-Speckled-Plumage (Horus) and come to rest in the south of Egypt in the Necropolis of Behdet, they gave birth to inhabitants for both Upper and Lower Egypt.[8]

The Divine Souls died in Edfu, where they were mummified and buried in a concealed place at the express command of Re; and from that moment on Egypt was blessed. These dead gods were the ancestors from whom all Egyptians sprang; and the Festival of Behdet was the means by which, every year, their burial places were kept safe. The annual visit of Horus and Hathor brought light and life to the Ancestors; and the ceremonies conducted at their graves brought prosperity to Egypt.

Certain rituals performed during the Feast of the Joyous Union and the Festival of Behdet are those normally associated with the ancient Egyptian Harvest Festival, which, throughout ancient Egyptian history, was celebrated not after the harvest was gathered in but as a preliminary to the period of reaping, on the first day of the First Month of Summer (the ninth month of the ancient Egyptian year). During the Ptolemaic Period at Denderah, the festival of Harsomtus (**colour plate 13**), the son of Horus and Hathor, was regarded as the harvest festival of the temple. It was celebrated in the First Month of Summer on the day of the New Moon and the four days following; and its rituals included treading on the burial mounds of the Divine Ancestors and the trampling underfoot of scattered grain. Similar rituals were performed during the harvest rites at Edfu and Kom Ombo, which were also celebrated during the First Month of Summer.

In Pharaonic times, the Harvest Festival was celebrated on the day of the Feast of the Coming Forth of Min, during which statues of Min,[9] the god of fertility, were carried out of their temples and displayed to the public. According to reliefs in the Memorial Temple of Ramesses III (1184-1153 BC) at Medinet Habu,[10] the high point of the ceremony came when the King, accompanied by the sacred white bull of Min, the Queen, statues of the royal ancestors and a statue of Min carried aloft on the shoulders of priests, made his way to an open field where he took a sickle and cut the first sheaf of emmer-wheat, signalling the beginning of the harvest. The rituals culminated in the releasing of four geese to the compass points with the announcement that Ramesses III had assumed the Double

37   Pronaos, *Edfu Temple, interior: 'Driving the Calves'*

Crown, although at Medinet Habu the geese are inexplicably portrayed in the relief as doves.

The Feast of the Joyous Union and the Festival of Behdet took place in the Third Month of Summer, two months after the Harvest Festival: yet harvest festival rites played a prominent part in the ceremonies, notably the offering of the first fruits of the field, which was celebrated twice, once when Hathor departed from Denderah and again on her arrival at Edfu; the offering of the field, the driving of the calves, the treading of the grave, which was performed twice, and the despatching of four geese to the compass points. Even the trampling of the King's enemies in the guise of fish can be equated to the trampling of the grain at harvest festival time. If it is puzzling why harvest festival rites were enacted out of harvest time, it may seem equally puzzling why some rites, such as the driving of the calves and the treading of the grave, should take place during Harvest Festival.

The driving of the calves (**37**) and the treading of the grave were the most significant rites in the Harvest Festival. The numerous scenes at Edfu of the driving of the calves[11] prove that this rite was originally a ceremonial threshing of grain, effected by driving four calves over the cut emmer-wheat in the presence of the King and the god of the harvest. The deity most associated with grain and agriculture was Osiris, who was murdered by his brother, Seth, but who triumphed over death to become King of the Underworld. His association with the concept of resurrection led to him being identified as the god of rebirth and regeneration through whose good offices the crops reappeared each year. Many Egyptian ceremonies were Osirianized, not least harvest ceremonies; and it is easy to understand how the ceremonial threshing of the corn came to be interpreted as the running of the calves over the grave of Osiris in order to obliterate all traces of it so that it should not be desecrated by the enemies of the god. The treading of the grave fulfilled a similar function. The grave was originally that of Osiris, the corn-god whose burial was enacted annually to ensure the fertility of the land. At Edfu, it was the graves belonging to the Ancestors which were trodden so that they, like Osiris, would ensure that Egypt was fecund.

The harvest festival ceremonies together with the sacred marriage that was embodied in the Feast of the Joyous Union and the ancestor cult that was celebrated in the Festival of Behdet were the means by which the King was reunited year by year with the forces of Nature, thereby obtaining the fertility that he passed on to his people, thus assuring them and the land on which they lived prosperity and abundance for the coming year.

10 The Festival of Victory

The Festival of Victory was celebrated from the twenty-first to the twenty-fifth day of the Second Month of Winter, that is, the sixth month of the ancient Egyptian year. Ideally, these dates correspond to 9-13 January in the Julian calendar, but in 110 BC, when the reliefs concerning the Festival of Victory were engraved in the Temple of Edfu, the civil and astronomical calendars were out of step, making the dates equivalent to 9-13 March. There are no inscriptions in Edfu Temple which list the ceremonies performed during the Festival; but on the inner surface of the western Enclosure Wall there is a series of three texts, known collectively as the Myth of Horus, which formed part of the Festival of Victory. These texts, which are long and accompanied by reliefs, are in the first and second registers on the wall. The former contains a version of the myth that was enacted annually as a sacred drama, entitled *The Triumph of Horus over his Enemies,*[1] which commemorated Horus' struggles against Seth, his final victory, his coronation as King of Upper and Lower Egypt and the triumphant dismemberment of his enemy. The latter contains the text now usually called *The Legend of the Winged Disk,*[2] a long and rather tedious account of the rivalry between Horus and Seth; and a much shorter text [3] which acts as an Appendix to *The Legend of the Winged Disk*.

The Triumph of Horus over his Enemies

Normally, the decoration of Edfu Temple develops from south to north, but some of the reliefs on the first two registers of the inner face of the western Enclosure Wall depart from this basic rule. The first register contains fifteen scenes, which for the purposes of this discussion will be called reliefs in order to distinguish them from the scenes in the drama. The reading of the register begins in the normal way with the first two reliefs at the southern end of the wall: but the following eleven reliefs only fall into a logical order if they are read from north to south. The last two reliefs in the register are again read in the normal way from south to north. Similarly with the sixteen reliefs in the second register: the first four are read from south to north, the following nine from north to south, the last three from south to north. This arrangement has the effect of isolating the reliefs read in reverse order from those on the rest of the wall.

In the first register, the eleven reliefs that are read in reverse order set out *The Triumph of Horus over his Enemies* as a drama in three Acts plus a Prologue and an

Epilogue. The first relief contains the Prologue; the next five contain Act One, Scenes 1 to 5; the seventh and eighth Act Two, Scenes 1 and 2; and the ninth to the eleventh Act Three, Scenes 1 to 3. In the top left hand corner of the eleventh relief is the text of the Epilogue, which has no relief of its own. The text of *The Triumph of Horus over his Enemies* is inscribed in long vertical columns on the left as one looks at each relief, filling the whole height of the register, except in the cases of Act Three, Scene 2, which has no vertical columns of inscription, and Act Three, Scene 3, in which the text is contained above the relief in four horizontal lines. The sculptured figures in each relief are on the right; and in every relief bar one (that containing Act Three, Scene 1) there is a long horizontal line of hieroglyphic inscription over the figures.

The reliefs containing the five Scenes in Act One depict Horus standing on a skiff, or canoe, which in real life would have been made of papyrus or wood, and in early times was used to hunt hippopotami in the marshes of the Delta. In each boat, Horus is accompanied by a demon with the head of an ape, a bull or a lion; and is in the act of spearing a hippopotamus with his harpoon. The relief depicting Act Two, Scene 1 is dominated by the great war-galley of Horus; and, like the relief depicting Act Two, Scene 2, in which Horus stands in his state barge, indicates action on water and on land. In the reliefs showing Act Three no boats are depicted, for in this Act the action takes place entirely on land. The identities of figures in the reliefs are given in short columns of hieroglyphs carved above their heads which contain their names and epithets. In the vertical columns containing the main text of the drama individual speeches are often not explicitly assigned to a character: in these cases, the identity of the speaker has to be deduced from what is said in the text. The play itself was more like a medieval miracle play than drama as it is known today. There was very little attempt at portraying individual character, or developing the action; and there was certainly no subtlety in the acting. Instead, characters in the drama took it in turns to at best declaim, at worst rant, a series of set speeches, many of which describe in bloodthirsty detail what is being done to the hippopotamus, which represents Horus' great enemy, Seth.

The Triumph of Horus over his Enemies was staged partly on and partly beside the temple's Sacred Lake, which represented for the purposes of the action the marshes of the Delta. Statues of Horus and Hathor, which had probably been carried out of their shrines in the temple with much pomp and ceremony some time before the drama was due to begin, were set in the place of honour beside the Lake. They were joined by an audience consisting of priests and laypeople. The chief participants in the drama were the King, ideally taking part in the play in person, a Reader, whose main task was to introduce the characters as they appeared 'on stage', masked priests impersonating various demons and deities, and a Chorus. The audience was encouraged to join the Chorus occasionally in shouting encouragement to Horus in his battles against Seth.

The Prologue opens with the Chorus singing the praises of Horus of Behdet, whose chief contribution to the drama is to rehearse the destruction he intends to

38   West Enclosure Wall, Edfu Temple: The Triumph of Horus, *Act I, Scene ii*

visit with his harpoon upon the Hippopotamus, Seth. Towards the end of the Prologue, the Chorus announces that 'here begins the bringing to pass of the triumph of Horus over his enemies as he hastens to slay his foes on sallying forth to battle'.[4] It ends with Chorus and audience exhorting Horus to hold tight to his harpoon. The five Scenes of Act One are devoted to the thrusting of ten harpoons into the body of the Hippopotamus. In Scene 1, the first harpoon is thrust into his snout, severing his nostrils, and the second into his forehead. In Scene 2, the third harpoon is stuck into his neck and the fourth into his head (**38**). In Scene 3, the fifth harpoon is thrust into his flank and the sixth into his ribs. In Scene 4, the seventh harpoon skewers the body of the Hippopotamus from his belly to his testicles and the eighth rips open his hind quarters. In Scene 5, the ninth harpoon strikes the legs of the Hippopotamus and the tenth is stuck into his hocks.

The whole of Act One is a playing out of the Harpoon Ritual, a survival of an ancient rite that celebrated the victory of a king over his enemies.[5] At regular intervals throughout the five Scenes of the Act the Chorus and onlookers encourage Horus in his actions by shouting the refrain 'hold tight!'; but there is no evidence that the protagonist was pitted against a real hippopotamus, even a very old or drugged animal! A model would have been used. In the reliefs, the sculpted hippopotami are much smaller than the human and divine figures; this, of course, was the conventional way of representing potentially harmful entities, which were always depicted on a smaller scale than the human figures in a relief

39   West Enclosure Wall, Edfu Temple: The Triumph of Horus, *Act II, Scene ii*

40   *West Enclosure Wall, Edfu Temple:* The Triumph of Horus, *Act III, Scene i*

41   *West Enclosure Wall, Edfu Temple:* The Triumph of Horus, *Act III, Interlude*

because of the belief that once the correct magical spells had been recited over the
relief the figures in it were brought to life. Between Scenes 4 and 5 of Act One
there is an Interlude in which another ancient ritual is enacted — the killing of
sabet-snakes, which symbolized the enemies of the falcon-god of Khem (Greek:
Letopolis). In the Pyramid Texts (*see* p. 138) the *sabet* were multi-coloured snakes,
possibly cobras, and at Khem they were beheaded and then eaten to symbolise the
destruction of the enemy.

Act Two is concerned with general rejoicing over the victory of Horus: in Scene
1 (**colour plate 14**), Horus and his children, the Young Harpooners, who have
been helping him, are praised; in Scene 2 (**39**), the people rejoice as Horus is
crowned and invested with the insignia of Kingship. In Act Three, victory is
celebrated by the dismemberment of the Hippopotamus. In Scene 1 (**40**), Isis
directs the dispatching of various parts of his body to the four corners of Egypt,
from Osiris in Busiris, who receives the foreleg, to Nephthys, who is given the
rump. The forepart and hindpart she claims for herself; and commands Horus to
'give his bones to the cat, his fat to the worms and his suet to the Young
Harpooners'. The Chorus and onlookers bring the Scene to an end with shouts
of 'Hold tight, Horus, hold tight!' after which there is a brief interlude (**41**)
before, in Scene 3 the Hippopotamus is dismembered for the second time (**42**).
The play ends with an Epilogue in which Horus is declared triumphant, having

42   West Enclosure Wall, Edfu Temple: The Triumph of Horus, *Act III, Scene iii*

overthrown the enemies of Osiris and Isis, of other gods and cities, and of Horus himself.

On the surface, *The Triumph of Horus over his Enemies* is the enactment of a mythological story, the struggle between two gods, Horus and Seth. The purpose of the drama, however, was to commemorate the victory of Horus over his enemies and his coronation as King of Upper and Lower Egypt; but since it was considered that Horus was embodied in the living King, the ultimate aim of the drama was to effect the downfall and destruction of the enemies of the King. Thus it was the King who was the alpha and omega of the play, securing the same triumph over his enemies that had been won by Horus and ensuring another year of peace and prosperity for himself, his land and its people.

Only one complete version of *The Triumph of Horus over his Enemies* has survived, and that is the copy engraved on the inner surface of the western Enclosure Wall (*see* p. 113). The wall was decorated during the reign of Ptolemy IX Soter II, probably about 110 BC, but quotations from the play scattered throughout Edfu Temple in parts that were constructed before the Enclosure Wall suggest that it was known at Edfu before that time. In the text of the play grammatical forms that were used during the New Kingdom, that is, some thousand years before the Ptolemaic temple was built, suggest that the Edfu version of *The Triumph of Horus over his Enemies* was an updated version of an earlier text. It may be that a scribe working in the Edfu Temple of the New Kingdom compiled a version of an even earlier play that he then deposited in the temple library. Certainly this was the claim made on the inner surface of the western Enclosure Wall on which the Ptolemaic version of the play was engraved, where it is written 'this wall is inscribed in conformity with the Emanations of Re'[6], that is, with material derived from ancient books.

In modern times, the French Egyptologists Étienne Drioton (1889-1961) and Maurice Alliot (1903-1960) denied that *The Triumph of Horus over his Enemies* was a play at all. Drioton omitted it from his major work on ancient Egyptian theatre,[7] and in a later book[8] claimed that the texts were simply a series of hymns intended for liturgical use. Alliot agreed with Drioton that *The Triumph of Horus over his Enemies* was not a play, although he did admit that it had dramatic overtones.[9] The English Egyptologists, Aylward Blackman (1883-1956) and Herbert Fairman (1907-1982) disagreed with the French scholars, and in their publication of the relevant texts[10] claimed that *The Triumph of Horus over his Enemies* was a sacred drama.

Professor Fairman was given the opportunity to test his theory in the early 1970s when the Head of the Drama Department at Padgate College of Education near Warrington in Cheshire asked one of his students, who happened to be Fairman's daughter, whether her father had any ancient Egyptian plays 'tucked away in a drawer at home'. The answer was 'Yes!' and on 23 June 1971 the Padgate College production of *The Triumph of Horus*[11] was given its premier. For the first time in nearly two thousand years this ancient Egyptian drama was heard, albeit in English translation; and Fairman's claim that it was indeed a play was vindicated.

The Legend of the Winged Disk

The second stage of the Festival of Victory, *The Legend of the Winged Disk*,[12] is not a drama but a long and tedious propagandist recital, full of puns on place-names and the actions of the gods, of various episodes in Horus' struggle against Seth. It is couched in the form of an historical document, and is even given a spurious mythological date, the 363rd year of the reign of the King of Upper and Lower Egypt, Re-Horakhty. In essence, the legend tells of how the inhabitants of Nubia (called Wawat, a pun on the Egyptian verb 'to conspire') began to plot sedition against Re, who commanded Horus of Behdet to deal with them. Horus flew up into the sky in the shape of a great winged sun-disk and shone so fiercely upon the rebels that they were blinded and in panic killed each other. In the guise of the Winged Disk, Horus pursued every enemy of Re until eventually he overthrew his greatest enemy, Seth. Horus cut off Seth's head and dragged him by his feet through the land, his spears sticking from his back; and in recognition of Horus' victory a winged disk was set up in every temple in every town in Egypt.

The purpose of *The Legend of the Winged Disk* is to support the claim of Horus of Behdet to supremacy; and to emphasise that he can and will protect the King. The text ends with the promise that a winged beetle will be placed on the breast of the King when danger threatens, and that the recitation of the magical spell written on the beetle will ensure that the King will be fearless and his enemies destroyed without delay. The spell written on the beetle is elaborated in the Appendix to *The Legend of the Winged Disk*. Its title refers to the presentation of a drink composed of grapes and water, but slaughtered ibex, oryx, long-horned and short-horned cattle, symbolic of the King's enemies, are also offered. The spell was designed to render the King's enemies powerless simply by declaring them to be so. They were then to be despatched to the north, south, east and west to become the different races of mankind, apart, of course, from the Egyptians.

The Legend of the Winged Disk was probably recited after performances of *The Triumph of Horus over his Enemies* as a final protective ritual. Together, the two sections of the Festival of Victory were designed to ensure the protection of the King and his triumph over his enemies, to secure for him, and therefore for Egypt, a prosperous reign, and to provide him with a written spell powerful enough to overcome all threats and dangers.

11 Kings and Ancestors

Throughout ancient Egyptian history, worship of the ancestors was inextricably bound up with Kingship. It is clear that although the royal line of descent was not unbroken every king of Egypt considered himself the direct descendant of previous kings,[1] whom he regarded as his 'ancestors'. It has been surmised that at some point in the making of a king, something happened which not only conferred divinity upon him but also linked him directly with all previous kings. By means of this procedure, Egypt achieved a remarkable stability that lasted for over three thousand years. The Egyptians accepted the Ptolemies as kings; and from an Egyptian viewpoint once the Ptolemies had become Pharaohs they were automatically linked with the divine Ancestors.

The worship of the Ancestors had always been a fundamental theme in Egyptian kingship; and ceremonies conducted on behalf of the Ancestors played an important part in many of the rituals celebrated in Edfu Temple — in the Daily Ritual, for instance, and in several of the great annual festivals such as the Feast of the Joyous Union, the New Year Festival and the Festival of Behdet. The top three registers on the east and west walls of the *Naos* exterior, however, are devoted to a single, great, Ancestral Ritual, the purpose of which was to ensure the perpetuation of the institution of Kingship. When this Ancestral/Kingship Ritual was celebrated it is impossible to say, for it does not appear in any of the lists of Calendar Festivals (*see* p. 93) celebrated at Edfu. Nor is it possible at this stage to determine where in the temple the Ritual was carried out; and it may simply have consisted of a procession of priests progressing along the Ambulatory and reciting the words of the Ritual without actually making any of the offerings featured in the rites depicted on the walls of the *Naos*.

The reliefs on the first registers on the east and west walls of the *Naos*[2] contain a related but nevertheless different ritual. Their layout, and that of the scenes in the second, third and fourth registers on these walls, follows the same pattern. Each scene on the registers of the west wall is matched by a similar scene on the east wall, with the west wall representing Lower Egypt and the east Upper Egypt. They are read horizontally from south to north along the register, beginning with the first scene on the west wall, in order to give Upper Egypt precedence over Lower Egypt (*see* p. 42), followed by the first scene on the east wall, and so on, reading alternately from west side to east side until the northern end of the wall is reached. On the west wall the divinity is always on the left of the scene with the King on the right; on the east wall the position is reversed. This arrangement

43   Naos, Edfu Temple: the King emerging from the Palace

allows the divinity always to face southward, looking in the direction of the main door of the temple, the desideratum of the sculptor (*see* p. 42) who would thereby ensure that a deity always had his or her face turned towards those who entered the temple.

The first scene in the first register on each wall is one showing the figure of a king emerging from the door of a palace, a necessary prelude to the performance of any ritual (**43**). Although the *cartouches* in this and several other scenes are blank, the majority of scenes in the register contain the *cartouches* of Ptolemy VIII Euergetes II, who dedicated the *Naos* in 142 BC. The second scene on each wall is one showing the gods, Horus and Thoth, purifying the King by pouring vases of water over him. Since water was the primordial element from which life came, in these scenes it falls from the vases in a shower of *ankhs*, the hieroglyphic signs symbolizing 'life'. This is the so-called 'Baptism of Pharaoh' (**colour plate 15**) which, it has been suggested, was not an act of simple purification such as any officiant must undergo before taking part in a temple ceremony but a rite which occurred on special occasions when the royal prerogatives were bestowed or confirmed.[3] The third scene on each wall depicts Nekhbet and Wadjet, tutelary goddesses of Upper and Lower Egypt, placing the Double Crown upon the head of the King (**44**); and the fourth scene shows him being led into into the temple by the co-templar deities (**45**). On the east wall, the King is flanked on one side

44   Naos, *Edfu Temple, east wall: Wadjet (left) and Nekhbet crowning the King*

45   Naos, *Edfu Temple, west wall: Induction of the King in the presence of Horus of
Behdet*

by Hathor and Atum and on the other by Montu and *Hor-sma-tawy*, son of Hathor
and Horus; on the west wall, *Hor-sma-tawy* is replaced by *Hor-pa-khred* , perhaps
better known by the Greek form of his name, Harpocrates, son of Isis and Osiris.
The fifth and sixth scenes on each wall, entitled 'Beholding the God', show the
King in the presence of Horus, an event so sacred that the inscriptions refer to the
King as 'the discreet one, who does not reveal what he had seen'[4]. The final scenes
in this section of the ritual are entitled 'Kissing the earth' and 'Adoring the God'.

The next two scenes on each wall are devoted to 'Spearing the Crocodile' and
'Slaying the Hippopotamus'. One of Seth's manifestations was as a crocodile;
hence by symbolically spearing the reptile the King was killing Seth and the evil
he represented. Seth was also symbolized by a hippopotamus; and 'Harpooning
the Hippopotamus' was an extremely ancient ritual, possibly dating to prehistoric
times. The King's speech in the scene of 'Spearing the Crocodile' is strongly
reminiscent in its wording of parts of *The Triumph of Horus over His Enemies* (*see* p.
115):

> I grasp my blade, I seize my spear. The heir am I of the Lord of Mesen
> (Horus of Behdet). I board my boat in the neighbourhood of the Pool
> of Horus. I kill the crocodiles, I stab the fiery-mouthed and ravening

crocodiles. I pierce their bodies. I slaughter their old ones and their young ones alike. I slay their females, I smash their eggs. I thrust the knife at the body of Meg (Seth). His meat pieces are given to the children of the fenmen.[5]

The following three scenes on each wall are rites of purification with water, natron and incense; these scenes are followed by one concerned with the offering of libations and four with the presentation of various kinds of food, meat and bread. In the eighteenth and last scene on each wall, the King 'offers the field' to Horus of Behdet, thereby presenting him with the agricultural land of Egypt in the hope of receiving the god's help in the performance of one of his prime royal duties, which was to ensure the fertility of the land.

Scenes showing the King 'Coming forth from the Palace' occur elsewhere in the temple: in the Inner and Outer Hypostyle Halls as preludes to Foundation Rituals (*see* p. 86); on the inner face of the Enclosure Wall; on the outer face of the western Enclosure Wall, again as a prelude to a Foundation Ritual; on the north wall of the *Naos* exterior; and in the *Mammisi*. Wherever these scenes introduce a Foundation Ritual they are never followed by scenes of baptism, crowning or induction into the presence of a god; but on the first register of the east and west exterior walls of the *Naos*, the scenes of 'Coming forth from the Palace', Baptism, Crowning and Induction are clearly linked with coronation rituals and are perhaps to be regarded as a renewal of kingship for the King, in which he was the recipient of rituals performed over him that enabled him to become an active participant, indeed the officiant, in the rites that feature in the remaining twenty-eight scenes. The ritual recorded on this part of the *Naos* was entirely concerned with the reigning King and was a prelude to the rites depicted on the remaining three registers of the east and west walls, which were intended to express the link between the living King and his Ancestors. Once the King had performed the introductory rites he was confirmed in his kingship, strengthened against his enemies and empowered to carry out the ritual depicted on the remaining three registers of the lateral walls of the *Naos* exterior.

Each of these registers [6] is divided into seventeen scenes in which the King is depicted as High Priest facing one or more deities and making an offering appropriate to each deity and to the rite with which the scene is concerned. In all cases the *cartouches* have been filled and name the King as Ptolemy VIII Euergetes II. In contrast to the scenes on the first register, and indeed throughout the temple, the scenes on the top three registers of the east and west walls of the *Naos* exterior are not read horizontally but vertically, and *boustrophedon* (lit: ox turning), that is, with alternate lines running contrary ways, as in ploughing.[7] There are one hundred and two scenes, many concerned with the offering of food and drink, and symbols of protection and purification or fertility and virility. Others depict the killing of enemies. These scenes are of no particular importance since the presentation of food and drink was an integral part of any temple ritual, and scenes of protection, purity and fertility are encountered in many Egyptian rituals, being

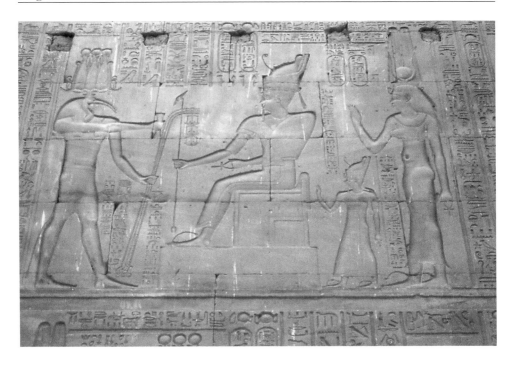

46   Naos, Edfu Temple: the royal family, in Greek dress, with the murdered prince
Memphites

considered essential to the well-being of Egypt. The scenes of killing enemies
fulfilled the same function.

The most important scenes are those that show the offering and receiving of
symbols of Kingship and the maintenance of order, and those that show the King
making offerings to ancestral deities. These are not the ancestral deities of the
temple who appear on the *Pronaos* as the *Shebtiw* (*see* p. 61) but the ancestors of the
world — the Great Ennead, the Little Ennead, the Ogdoad and the Fourteen Kas
of Re, together with the nine ancestral deities of Edfu Temple. The King is also
depicted making offerings to his own immediate Ptolemaic ancestors in the three
scenes in each register that lie third from the northern end of each wall. In the two
scenes on the second register of each wall Thoth is shown in the first inscribing
on a palm-stick the years of reign allotted to Ptolemy VIII Euergetes II and in the
second proffering him the *mks*, that is, the cylindrical container that held the title
deeds to the kingdom. In these scenes Euergetes II is accompanied by his sister-
wife Cleopatra II and their son, Memphites (**46**), who had been born in 144 BC,
two years before the *Naos* of Edfu Temple was dedicated. Memphites was
murdered on his father's orders in 132 BC (*see* p.27) but no attempt seems to have
been made to expunge his image from the temple wall.

In the scene on the third register of the west wall the King is shown presenting
ointment and raiment to his parents, Ptolemy V Epiphanes and Cleopatra I.

Although deceased, they are not depicted in mummiform shape but are dressed in normal Egyptian costume, with Epiphanes seated upon a throne, the Queen standing behind it, both facing their son. In the corresponding scene on the east wall the Queen named in the *cartouche* is not Cleopatra, the wife of Epiphanes, who appeared in the previous scene, but Berenice. The founder of the Dynasty, Ptolemy I Soter I, was married to a Berenice, as was Ptolemy III Euergetes I, the great-grandfather of Euergetes II. Which, if either, of these two queens appears in the scene under discussion is not clear. It is possible that 'Berenice' was simply written in mistake for 'Cleopatra'; but in a similar set of scenes in the *Pronaos* interior,[8] it is Ptolemy III Euergetes I who appears alongside Berenice, which may mean that the mistake lay in placing Epiphanes in the scene.

In the scene on the fourth register of the west wall of the *Naos* exterior Euergetes II is shown offering incense and libation to his great-great-grandfather, Ptolemy II Philadelphus, and his sister-wife, Arsinoe II, although it was Philadelphus' first wife, Arsinoe I, who was actually the great-great-grandmother of Euergetes II. On the east wall, Ptolemy IV Philopator and Arsinoe III, the grandparents of Euergetes II, are depicted receiving the offering. It is obvious that in these and the preceding two scenes, Euergetes II is making offerings, all of a suitably funerary nature, to his Royal Ancestors. They are the second Ptolemy to the fifth, together with their queens. Surprisingly, the founder of the Dynasty, Ptolemy I Soter I, is not represented. Neither is Ptolemy VI Philometor, Euergetes' elder brother, who died in 145 BC; nor, not unexpectedly, is Ptolemy VII Neos Philopator, the son of Philometor, who reigned briefly in 145 BC before being disposed of by his uncle, Euergetes II.

The most unusual feature of the two scenes on the second register is the fact that the male members of the royal family are dressed in Greek costume. The depiction on the wall of a temple of a Ptolemaic King dressed in Greek costume was very rare. Apart from the two on the Naos, there are two in the interior of the Sanctuary and one on the east Enclosure Wall. In all five scenes the King is the recipient of offerings; he is never portrayed in Greek costume when making the offerings. In three of the scenes, Thoth is inscribing his years of reign, in the fourth the King is offered life by Thoth and in the fifth he is offered the testament by Horus. There are many other examples of this type of kingship scene throughout the temple but in none of them has it been considered necessary to depict the King wearing Greek costume. One is drawn to the conclusion that in showing the King in Greek dress the designer of the relief was endeavouring to make a point (*see* p.130).

The Ptolemies took on the role of god-king only gradually. The first Ptolemy did not subscribe to the notion at all, the second conformed to Egyptian custom by taking the five titles of the Royal Titulary, and by marrying his full sister, a custom totally alien to Greek ideas. Ptolemy IV Philopator, likewise, made this concession to Egyptian custom and married his sister, as did almost all of his successors. From his time onwards, the Ptolemaic kings were weak; and during the latter half of the three centuries of the Dynasty they were especially so, constantly indulging in quarrels amongst themselves and making challenges for the throne. They turned to the priesthood for support (*see* p.23).

By the time the *Naos* of Edfu Temple was built, the Ptolemaic kings had accepted the necessity of cooperating with the powerful Egyptian priesthood. Ptolemy VIII Euergetes II must have been very willing to allow himself to be depicted in an ancestral ritual, thus demonstrating his legitimacy as king and, perhaps more importantly, the legitimacy of the Ptolemaic Dynasty, reaffirming its right to govern Egypt. By worshipping his Ancestors he established a link between himself and those who had been kings of Egypt since time immemorial. From the point of view of the priesthood, this was a desirable thing. It did not matter to them that the king whose legitimacy was being proclaimed on the *Naos* of Edfu Temple was a Macedonian, a foreigner, a fact that is made abundantly clear in the scenes in which Euergetes II is depicted wearing Greek dress (*see* p.129). To the priests of Egypt, especially those devoted to Horus, the royal god *par excellence*, it was Kingship itself and not any individual king that was all-important. They tolerated the Ptolemaic kings partly because the kings supported them but largely because they had a connection, however tenuous, with Alexander the Great. But the priests were bent upon maintaining the concept of Kingship in the belief that by doing so they were preserving Egypt against the day when the 'Ionian dogs' and all foreigners would be driven out and the Kingship handed to a true, native-born King.

12 Postscript

Loss and Recovery of Edfu Temple

Even before the Emperor Justinian closed down all the pagan temples in the early sixth century AD, Edfu had probably been abandoned by its priests. The temple, denuded of its wooden and metal furnishings, and all portable objects, and with the doors no longer in position to keep out blown sand, and no sweeper-priests to brush it away, began to silt up. Gradually, the local inhabitants moved into the temple, which provided them with living quarters that were in many ways superior to their small mud-brick houses. Sadly, where soot and grease from cooking fires did not blacken the walls and ceilings, and dirt and misuse damage the fabric of the building, the reliefs on the walls were damaged deliberately through superstition and fear of the evil eye (**47**). The Egyptians had long believed that the sculpted or painted image had a capacity for malevolence, and made the temple safe for their occupation by chiselling out the figures on the walls; and as the floor levels within the temple became higher because of the accumulated rubbish and sand, so more reliefs came within easy reach. With the coming of first Chrisianity and then Islam, the pagan reliefs were damaged through religious fervour; and in the case of the Muslim occupants of the temple because Islam does not approve of the artistic representation of the human figure.

The wonderful antiquities of ancient Egypt were brought to the attention of the modern western world after Napoleon's Expedition to Egypt in 1798. Unfortunately, the attention was mostly that of treasure hunters and antique collectors, and it was not until the French Egyptologist, Auguste Mariette (1821-1881), convinced the Khedive, Said Pasha, of the necessity of persuading people that ancient monuments needed care and conservation rather than exploitation and expropriation that the situation was brought under control. Mariette created the first Egyptian National Antiquities Service and founded a museum in an old house at Boulaq in Cairo that was the forerunner of the great Egyptian Museum of today; and in 1858, he was appointed Director of Egyptian Monuments.

In 1860, Mariette began the clearance of Edfu Temple, which he had found in a deplorable condition (**48**, **49; colour plate 16**). It had been turned into a veritable village, filled with stables and storehouses of every kind, with the roof of the *Naos* covered in mud-brick houses, and the inner chambers filled with rubbish almost to the ceiling. He described how he went about the task: 'I arranged the demolition of the sixty-four houses that encumbered the roof, as

47   *Sanctuary, Edfu Temple: mutilated relief of Horus of Behdet*

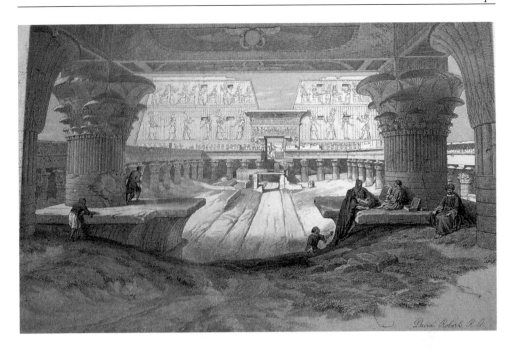

48   *Edfu Temple in AD 1834: view from* Pronaos *into Forecourt. Lithograph by David Roberts*

49   *Edfu Temple in 1857. Photograph by Francis Frith*

133

50   *Edfu Temple in the 1930s: Pylon Gateway, West Enclosure Wall
and the top of the* Pronaos

well as twenty-eight more that approached too near the outer wall of the temple.'
Once the temple had been cleared (**50**), it was possible for the Egyptian
Antiquities Service to undertake important conservation work, rebuilding unsafe
walls and repairing the roof. The Temple of Edfu, once painted in bright colours
but now mellowed to a creamy-brown, stood revealed in all its glory, its wealth of
inscriptions ready to give up their secrets to those who could read them — at that
time, no one!

It was less than forty years since Jean-François Champollion (1790-1832) had
announced, in 1822, that he had succeeded in deciphering ancient Egyptian
hieroglyphs. The inscriptions at Edfu, however, are not written in the sort of
hieroglyphic writing that Champollion had mastered, but in a special script
known today as 'Ptolemaic writing'. Several nineteenth-century scholars worked
on Ptolemaic texts, notably the German, Johannes Dümichen (1833-1894),
whose chief interest was in the inscriptions in the Temple of Hathor at Denderah;
the Swiss, Édouard Naville (1844-1926), who first visited Egypt in 1865 to copy
inscriptions at Edfu; and the Swede, Karl Piehl (1853-1904), who made the study
of Ptolemaic texts in general his speciality. Real progress was not made in the
study of Ptolemaic until the twentieth century, in particular by the French
scholars Étienne Drioton (1889-1961) and Maurice Alliot (1903-1960), and the
English philologists Aylward Blackman (1883-1956) and Herbert Fairman (1907-
1982), with Alliot, Blackman and Fairman making the study of the Edfu
inscriptions their particular area of expertise.

The task of the twentieth-century philologists was made easier by the
publication in book form of all the inscriptions in Edfu Temple by two French
Egyptologists: Maxence, Marquis de Rochemonteix (1849-1891) and Émile
Chassinat (1868-1948). Shortly before his death, de Rochemonteix began the
publication of the inscriptions under the title *Le Temple d'Edfou*, part one of which
was issued posthumously in 1892. Chassinat continued the mammoth task, which
was not completed until 1934, by which time there were fourteen volumes with
over 3000 pages, each measuring 32cm by 23cm, and plates (**51**). It has been
claimed that this is probably the most magisterial publication ever produced by a
single Egyptologist.

Ptolemaic Writing

The temples of Edfu, Denderah, Philae, Esna and Kom Ombo, built during the
Ptolemaic Dynasty, are some of the most important in Egypt. They hold an
especially important place in any study of ancient Egyptian temples for three main
reasons: they were erected over a comparatively short space of time and can be
seen as entities in themselves rather than as sprawling masses such as the edifices
at Karnak, which were enlarged and embellished over hundreds of years; Edfu,
Denderah and Philae are the best preserved temples in Egypt; and they all hold a
great deal of information about Egyptian mythology and religious ritual in their
inscriptions, recording in detail the ceremonies celebrated in the temple. Much of

*51   East Enclosure Wall, Edfu Temple, interior: dado with Ptolemaic writing:
example of a Chassinat plate*

the information contained in the inscriptions is unavailable from other sources.

The inscriptions in Ptolemaic temples are more extensive than those in the temples of earlier periods, but were done in such a deliberately elaborate and confusing hieroglyphic script that only a select few were able to read them. This allowed the priests to use temple walls as source books in stone of Egyptian temple ritual, confident that only those entitled to a knowledge of the rituals would be trained to read the inscriptions. The use of such a specialized script may be thought excessively cautious since throughout Egyptian history writing had been the exclusive preserve of the scribal class, with most Egyptians unable to read or write. In any case, for some four hundred years before the Ptolemies arrived in Egypt, the normal writing of everyday business and legal life had been demotic, a very much abbreviated version of the cursive script, hieratic, that had sometimes been used instead of hieroglyphs, making the knowledge of hieroglyphs even more esoteric. The priests of the Ptolemaic era, however, made sure that even those who would normally expect to be able to read hieroglyphs would find difficulty with Ptolemaic writing.

Obviously, any script used in the Macedonian Greek period of Egyptian history could be called Ptolemaic: but the adjective has been specialized to describe the system of writing employed in the inscriptions found in the temples of the Graeco-Roman period. The language in these inscriptions is one that was dead

52   *Sanctuary, Edfu Temple: facade showing Ptolemaic writing*

even at the time they were being written: it is not the contemporary spoken language of the native Egyptians but a priestly revival of a much older stage of ancient Egyptian, with roots firmly in the Pyramid Texts, the inscriptions found in several pyramids of the Fifth and Sixth Dynasties (*c.* 2400 to 2180 BC), making them the oldest-known body of religious literature, which itself dates back to before 3000 BC when the age of writing began. Many Ptolemaic inscriptions contain old grammatical forms, constructions and vocabulary, due no doubt to a nationalistic trend towards archaizing that had begun under the non-Egyptian Kushite kings of the Twenty-fifth Dynasty (716-664 BC) and continued with zest by the kings of the first Saite Dynasty (664-525 BC). Several inscriptions in the Ptolemaic temples even preserve examples of old theology and mythology that are otherwise lost.

Ptolemaic writing is a richly decorative script that has taken the hieroglyphic signs used in writing classic Egyptian and added to them. It has given some of these signs new meanings and values, and increased the number of ideograms used. Compared with classic Egyptian, Ptolemaic uses a great number of purely alphabetic signs, possibly in a deliberate attempt to indicate the current pronounciation of words. In Ptolemaic, there was a revival of archaic spellings, and also a variety of alternatives for well-known signs, values and spellings.

Each Ptolemaic temple has its own variations in writing. The earliest and best Ptolemaic writing is found in Edfu Temple (**52**), the latest at Esna, whilst Denderah has the most decorative. Esna has the most difficult script — there are over eighty different ways of writing *n*, for example; and even at Edfu, which has a less difficult script, there are over 7000 signs in use — classic Egyptian has about 800. Ptolemaic in its fully-developed and most decorative stage was rarely used. The majority of the inscriptions in Ptolemaic temples can be read relatively straightforwardly, almost as though they were in classic Egyptian, albeit perhaps more decoratively written and with phonetic changes in the language indicated. Fully developed Ptolemaic was usually reserved for those parts of a temple that catch the eye — along the bottom of a wall, for instance, or beneath the frieze at the top, on doorframes, architraves, ceilings and columns, and in the writing of divine titles and epithets. Even so, many Ptolemaic inscriptions remain undeciphered, their secrets yet to be discovered.

Bibliography and Further Reading

Abbreviations

BIFAO	Bulletin de l'Institut Français d'Archéologie Orientale
BJRL	Bulletin of the John Rylands Library (Manchester)
Chr. d'Ég.	Chronique d'Égypte
JEA	Journal of Egyptian Archaeology
JMEOS	Journal of the Manchester Egyptian and Oriental Society
JWCI	Journal of the Warburg and Courtauld Institutes
ZAS	Zeitschrift fur ägyptische Sprache und Altertumskunde

1 Historical Background

Arrian.	*The Campaigns of Alexander*, Penguin Classics, 1971
Bevan, E.R.	*A History of Egypt under the Ptolemaic Dynasty*, London, 1927
Bowman, A.K.	*Egypt after the Pharaohs*, London, 1986
Elgood, P.G.	*The Ptolemies of Egypt*, Bristol, 1938
Green, P.	*Alexander the Great*, London, 1970
Hallett, L.H-.	*Cleopatra: Histories, Dreams and Distortions,* London, 1990
Renault, M.	*The Nature of Alexander*, London, 1975

2 The Mythology of Horus

Gardiner, A.H.	'Horus the Behdetite' in *JEA*, 30, 1944, pp.23-60
Griffiths, J.G.	*The conflict of Horus and Seth,* Liverpool, 1960
Watterson,B.	*Gods of Ancient Egypt*, Stroud, 1996

3 Egyptian Temples and their Decoration

Badawy, A.	'The architectural symbolism of the *mammisi*-chapels in Egypt', in *Chr. d'Ég.*, XXXVIII, No.75, Jan. 1963,

	pp.78-90
Barb, A.A.	'Mystery, myth and magic', in *The Legacy of Egypt* (ed. J.R. Harris), 2nd ed., Oxford, 1971
Daumas, F.	*Les* mammisis *des temples égyptiens*, Paris, 1958
Emery, W.B.	*Archaic Egypt,* Harmondsworth, 1961
Gardiner, A.H.	*The tomb of Amenemhat (No. 82)*, London, 1915
Jelínková, E.A.E.	'The *Shebtiw* in the temple at Edfu', in *ZAS*, 87, 1962, pp.41-54
Jéquier, G.	'Les temples primitifs et la persistance des types archaïques dans l'architecture religieuse', in *BIFAO*, 6, 1908, pp.25-41
Nelson, H.H.	'The significance of the temple in the ancient Near East. 1: the Egyptian temple', in *The Biblical Archaeologist,* VII (3), 1944, pp.44-53
Reymond, E.A.E.	*The mythological origin of the Egyptian temple,* Manchester, 1969.
Wit, C. de.	'Les inscriptions des lions-gargouilles du temple d'Edfou' in *Chr. d'Ég.*, 29, 1954, pp.29-45.

4 The Temple of Horus at Edfu

Blackman, A.M.	'The House of the Morning', in *JEA*, 5, 1918, pp.148-165.
Cauville, S.	*Edfou,* Cairo 1984.
Cauville, S.	*La théologie d'Osiris / Edfou*, Cairo, 1983.
Cauville, S. and Devauchelle, D.	
	'Les mesures réelles du Temple d'Edfou', in *BIFAO,* 84, 1984. pp. 23-34.
Chassinat, E.	*Le mammisi d'Edfou*, Cairo, 1910.
Daumas, F.	*Les* mammisis *des temples égyptiens*, Paris, 1958.
Gardiner, A.H.	'The Baptism of Pharaoh', in *JEA*, 36, 1950, pp.3-12. Addendum in *JEA*, 37, 1951, p.111.
Wit, C. de.	'Les inscriptions dédicatoires du Temple d'Edfou', in *Chr. d'Ég.*, 36, 1961, pp. 56-97 (EIV, 1-16) and pp. 277 320 (EVII, 1-20).
Wit, C. de.	'Les inscriptions des lions-gargouilles du temple d'Edfou', in *Chr. d'Ég.*, 29, 1954, pp. 29-45.

5 Priesthood and the Daily Ritual

| Alliot, M. | *Le culte d'Horus / Edfou au temps des Ptolemées,* 2 vols., Cairo, 1954. |

Blackman, A.M. *Gods, priests and men: Studies in the religion of Pharaonic Egypt* (ed. A.B. Lloyd), London, 1997.

Blackman, A.M. 'The sequence of episodes in the Egyptian daily temple liturgy', in *JMEOS*, 8, 1919, pp.27-53.

Blackman, A.M. & Fairman, H.W.
 'A group of texts inscribed on the facade of the Sanctuary in the Temple of Horus at Edfu', in *Miscellanea Gregoriana*, Rome, 1941, pp.397-428.

Herodotus, *The Histories*, Penguin Classics.

Lefebvre, G. *Histoires des grands prêtres d'Amon de Karnak jusqu'la XXIe Dynastie*, Paris, 1929.

Moret, A. *Le rituel du culte divin journalier en Egypte*, Paris, 1902.

Sauneron, S. *The priests of ancient Egypt*, New York, 1960.

6 The Foundation and Consecration of Edfu Temple

Blackman, A.M. and Fairman, H.W.
 'The Consecration of an Egyptian Temple According to the Use of Edfu', in *JEA*, 32, 1946, pp.75-91.

Fairman, H.W. 'Worship and festival in an Egyptian temple', in *BJRL*, 37, 1954, pp.165-203.

7 The New Year Festival

Alliot, M. *Le culte d'Horus / Edfou au temps des Ptolemées*, Vol.1, Cairo, 1954.

8 The Installation of the Sacred Falcon

Alliot, M. *Le culte d'Horus / Edfou au temps des Ptolemées.*, Vol. 2, Cairo, 1954.

Blackman, A.M. 'The King of Egypt's Grace Before Meat', in *JEA*, 31, 1945.

Frankfort, H. 'State Festivals in Egypt and Mesopotamia', in *JWCI*, 15, 1952.

Ibrahim, M. *Aspects of Egyptian kingship according to the inscriptions of the Temple of Edfu*, Cairo, 1966.

9 The Feast of the Joyous Union

Blackman, A.M. and Fairman, H.W.
    'The Significance of the Ceremony 'hwt bhsw' in the Temple of Horus at Edfu' in *JEA*, 35, 1949, pp.98-112 and *JEA*, 36, 1950, pp.63-81.
Gauthier, H.   *Les fêtes du dieu Min*, Cairo, 1934.
Murnane, W.J.   *United with Eternity: a Concise Guide to the Monuments of Medinet Habu*, Cairo, 1980.
Watterson, B.   *Women in Ancient Egypt*, Stroud, 1991.

10 The Festival of Victory

Alliot, M.   *Le culte d'Horus / Edfou au temps des Ptolemées*, Vol. 2, Cairo, 1954.
Blackman, A.M. and Fairman, H.W.
    'The Myth of Horus at Edfu II: The Triumph of Horus over his Enemies — A Sacred Drama',in *JEA*, XXVIII, 32-38, 1942; *JEA*, XXIX, 2-36, 1943; *JEA*, XXX, 5-22, 1944.
Drioton, E.   'Le texte dramatique d'Edfou', in *Cahiers des Annales de Service des Antiquitiés de l'Égypte*, no. 11, Cairo, 1948.
Drioton, E.   *Le Théatre égyptien*, Paris, 1942.
Fairman, H.W.   'The Myth of Horus at Edfu I: The Legend of the Winged Disk', in *JEA*, 21, 1935, pp.26-36.
Fairman, H.W.   *The Triumph of Horus*, London, 1974.
Säve-Söderbergh, T.   *On Egyptian Representations of Hippopotamus Hunting as a Religious Motive*, Uppsala, 1953.

11 Kings and Ancestors

Fairman, H.W.   'The Kingship rituals of Egypt', in *Myth, Ritual and Kingship* (ed. S.H. Hooke), Oxford, 1958, pp.74-104.
Frankfort, H.   *Kingship and the gods*, Chicago, 1948.
Reymond, E.A.E.   'Worship of the Ancestor Gods at Edfu' in *Chr. d'Ég.*, 38, 1963, pp.49-70.
Watterson, B.   *An ancestral ritual from Edfu Temple: an investigation of inscriptions on the* Naos *exterior.* Ph. D. thesis presented to the University of Liverpool, 1976.

12 Postscript

Fairman, H.W.   'Notes on the alphabetic signs employed in the hieroglyphic inscriptions of the Temple of Edfu' in *Ann. Serv.*, 43, 1943, pp.191-318.

Fairman, H.W.   'Ptolemaic notes', in *Ann. Serv.*, 44, 1944, pp.263-278.

References

Quotations from Chassinat's *Le Temple d'Edfou* give volume, page and line numbers in the following manner: EIV, 10, 2, that is, volume IV, page 10, second line on page.

1 Historical Background

1   'Mr Lely, I desire you would use all your skill to paint my picture truly like me, and not flatter me at all; but remark all these roughnesses, pimples, warts, and everything as you see me, otherwise I will never pay a farthing for it.' Oliver Cromwell in Horace Walpole's *Anecdotes of Painting in England,* Chapter 12.
2   Justin, Book XXXVIII, Chapter 8.

3 Egyptian Temples and their Decoration

1   Emery, 1961, p.52.
2   Jéquier, 1905, pp.25-41.
3   Reymond, 1969, Chapter 2.
4   Jelinková, 1962.
5   Nelson, 1944, pp.44-53.
6   EVIII, 91, 15-92, 2.
7   Barb, 1971, pp. 138-169.
8   For example, EIV, 6, 9.
9   EVII, 12, 6.

4 The Temple of Horus at Edfu

1   EIV, 1-16.
2   EVII, 1-20.
3   EIV, 4, 7-8.

4   EVII, 11, 8-12, 2.
5   EVII, 19, 6.
6   EVII, 19, 7.
7   EVII, 19, 8
8   EVII, 19, 3-4.
9   EVII, 18, 10-19, 1.
10   EVII, 19, 1-2.
11   EVII, 8, 3.
12   EVII, 9, 4.
13   EX, Pls CXXIII-CXXV; CXXVIII-CXXX & EV, 12-28; 105-124.
14   EV, 183-200.
15   EV, 87-103.
16   EVII, 17, 12.
17   ibid.
18   Blackman, 1918.
19   EIII, 347 and 351.
20   EIII, 339, 9-10.
21   EVII, 17, 4-5.
22   EIV, 13, 14-14, 1.
23   EVII, 17, 5-6.
24   EVII, 17, 10.
25   EVII, 16, 6.
26   EVII, 16, 7-8
27   EVII, 16, 8
28   EVII, 15, 7-8
29   EVII, 15, 5
30   EIV, 5, 11.
31   EIV, 13, 7.
32   EIV, 5, 1.
33   EIV, 5, 3.
34   EIV, 13, 10.
35   Alliot, 1954, i, pp.314-325.
36   EVII, 13, 3.
37   EIV, 5, 5.
38   Watterson, 1996, p. 70.
39   EVII, 13, 4.
40   EIV, 5, 8.
41   EIV, 15, 4-7.

5 Priesthood and the Daily Ritual

1   Herodotus, II, 38.
2   ibid.

3   Plutarch, *De Iside et Osiride,* 72.
4   Herodotus, II, 37.
5   op. cit. 40.
6   Lefebvre, 1929, p. 132 foll.
7   EIII, 361.
8   EIV, 343-44.
9   Blackman, 1919.
10   EI, 24, 16-26, 15; 30, 12-31, 16; 36, 3-37, 6. EXI, Pls CCXIII-CCXIV;
     CCIX-CCXX. EI, 40, 3-42, 2; 44, 19-45; 48, 10-49, 19. EXI, Pls
     CCXXII-CCXXIV
11   EI, 20, 1-3.
12   EVIII, 58, 14-15.
13   EII, 139, 8.
14   *See* M. Lichtheim, *Ancient Egyptian Literature,* Volume II, Berkeley, 1996,
     p. 119 foll.
15   EI, pp. 13-20.
16   Blackman & Fairman, 1941.
17   EI, 26, 4-6.
18   EVII, 18, 3-4.
19   EVI, 105, 2-3; EVII, 83, 16-84, 2; 207, 7-10; 239, 2-4.
20   EIII, 356, 1.
21   EI, 282, 12-15.

6 The Foundation and Consecration of Edfu Temple

1   EVII, 42, 8-57, 7; EIX, Pls CLXIII & CLXV.
2   EII, 29, 9-34; 59, 5-64, 2; EIX, Pl. XL b-e.
3   EIII, 102, 9-112, 5; EIX, Pls LVIII & LXI.
4   EIII, 112, 8-117, 8; 165, 3-170, 1; EIX, Pls LXII & LXIV.
5   F. L. Griffith, *The Inscriptions of Siut and Der Rifeh,* Pls 6, 277-8; 7, 297.
6   Griffith, *op. cit.,* PL. 7, 298.
7   EIV, 330-331.

7 The New Year Festival

1   EI, 359, 15-18; EXII, Pl. 324; EV, 397, 5-401, 5; EV, 394, 10-395, 7; EXIII,
     Pls 489, 490, 491. See also Alliot, *Culte,* Vol. 1.
2   EV, 163, 17-164, 1 & 164, 6-7.
3   EV, 399, 1-6; EVI, 9, 7-8.
4   EV, 397, 6.
5   EI, 553, 15-554, 1.

8 The Installation of the Sacred Falcon

1   EVI, 92, 13-18; 93, 2-99, 16; 100, 2-104, 7; 143, 8-10; 143, 12-152, 12;
    152, 14-157, 2; 262, 5-9; 262, 11-269, 12; 269, 14-274, 7; 297, 12-17;
    298, 2-304, 12; 305, 2-309, 7.
2   EVI, 102, 3-103, 6.
3   EVI, 102, 5.
4   EVI, 102, 5.
5   EVI, 102, 5-8.
6   EVI, 93, 11.
7   EVI, 102, 9.
8   EVIII, 109, 11-110, 6 (west wing, east face) and EVIII, 148, 2-12
    (east wing, west face).
9   Ibrahim, 1966, p.95 foll.
10 Blackman, 1945.
11 EVI, 305, 2-4.
12 Frankfort, 1952, p.8.
13 EVI, 103, 4-5.
14 Blackman, 1945, p.70.

9 The Feast of the Joyous Union

1   EV, 29, 9-33, 16; 34, 2-35, 3; 124, 8-129, 11; 130, 17-136, 4.
2   EVII, 26, 9-12.
3   EV, 30, 3-6.
4   Watterson, 1991, p.59.
5   EIV, 3, 5-8.
6   EV, 134, 2.
7   EI, 173, 3-174, 7; EI, 382, 4-15; EII, 51, 3-52, 8; EIII, 323, 5-12; EIV, 102,
    17-103, 13; EIV, 239, 13-241, 14; EV, 61, 17-63, 16; EV, 160, 12-162, 6;
    EVII, 118, 4-119, 8; EVII, 279, 16-281, 2.
8   EIV, 240, 6-9.
9   Gauthier, 1934.
10 Murnane, 1980, pp.32-38
11 Blackman and Fairman, 1949 & 1950.

10 The Festival of Victory

1   EVI, 60, 6-90.
2   EVI, 108, 15-132, 5.
3   EVI, 132, 7-136, 9.
4   EVI, 61, 2-3

5   Säve-Söderbergh, 1953, pp.25-41.
6   EVI, 14, 12-13.
7   Drioton, 1942.
8   Drioton, 1948.
9   Alliot, 1954, pp. 677-822.
10   Blackman and Fairman, 1942-44.
11   Fairman, 1974.
12   Fairman, 1935.

11 Kings and Ancestors

1   Fairman, 1958, p.77.
2   West wall: EIV, 49, 10-68, 13; east wall: EIV, 202, 4-224, 14;
     EX, Pls LXXXIV-LXXXVII
3   Gardiner, 1950, p.6.
4   EIV, 55, 2.
5   EIV, 211, 8-212, 4.
6   Register II, west: EIV, 76, 5-95, 3; east: EIV, 233, 8-251, 5.
     Register III, west: EIV, 102, 4-125, 7; east: EIV, 257, 13-281, 9.
     Register IV, west: EIV, 134, 6-151, 3; east: 290, 4-307, 6.
     Plates: west: EX, XC-XCIII; east: LXXXIV-LXXXVII.
7   Watterson, 1976, p.149 foll.
8   EIX, Pls LXI & LXIII.

Index